TWAYNE'S WORLD AUTHORS SERIES
A Survey of the World's Literature

WEST INDIES

Joseph Jones, University of Texas, Austin

EDITOR

West Indian Poetry

TWAS 422

WEST INDIAN POETRY

By LLOYD W. BROWN
University of Southern California

TWAYNE PUBLISHERS
A DIVISION OF G. K. HALL & CO., BOSTON

Library of Congress Cataloging in Publication Data

Brown, Lloyd Wellesley, 1938 -
  West Indian poetry.

  (Twayne's world authors series; TWAS 422: West
Indies)
  Bibliography: p. 183 - 90.
  Includes index.
  1. West Indian poetry (English) — History and
criticism. I. Title.
PR9212.B7   811'.009   77 - 21613
ISBN 0-8057-6262-0

In Memory
of
Clarence G. Webb-Harris

Contents

About the Author

Lloyd W. Brown is Professor of Comparative Literature at the University of Southern California. Originally from Jamaica, he graduated from the University of the West Indies. He then emigrated to Canada where he did his graduate work and taught before entering the United States. He is the author of *Bits of Ivory: Narrative Techniques in Jane Austen's Fiction* (Louisiana State University Press, 1973), and has edited a collection of essays, *The Black Writer in Africa and the Americas* (Hennessey & Ingalls, 1973). He has also written numerous articles on English and American literatures, and on Black literatures, in European, North American, and Caribbean journals.

Preface

Most of West Indian literature, that is the literature of the English-speaking Caribbean, originates with Guyana and the three major islands, Barbados, Jamaica, and Trinidad-Tobago. Historically this is obvious enough. But what has always been uncertain has been the basis on which we have traditionally assigned the corporate identity of a single national literature, "West Indian literature," to writings from territories which have always fostered a sense of separateness (even divisive insularity at times), and which have become separate and sovereign nations since 1962. The criticism of West Indian literature has therefore been based on the paradox of a national literature developed and shared by separate nations. And a major effect of this paradox has been the continuing attempt to develop approaches that describe those common assumptions and experiences which constitute a kind of national consciousness in this literature. Some critics, notably Robert Hamner in his recent study of V. S. Naipaul[1] and Cameron King and Louis James in their collection on West Indian literature,[2] tend to dismiss such an attempt by arguing that the literature and its culture are really extensions of a European tradition. There is no denying that in many crucial respects West Indian literature is an outgrowth of the Western literary tradition. But what is questionable is the notion that this outgrowth is simply an offspring that needs to be enclosed by the solicitous expansion of a paternalistic Western criticism. We need to avoid oversimplifications of West Indian literature as a mere extension of English literature, in much the same way that we should question equally suspect definitions of that literature in exclusively non-Western terms.

This need is rooted in two related aspects of West Indian literary history. First the hybrid nature of West Indian culture and history cannot accommodate the tidy, exclusive identity of the Western "offspring." Of course the exclusive Western label could apply to the kind of literary perspective which sought to treat the discrete sources of West Indian society as if they were all part of a homogenous Western experience. And this is the kind of homogenizing perspective which critics like King and James profess

to find in the literature: "the greatest writers in . . . the West Indies, have been those who have been able most fully" to come to
terms with their situation "through mastery of the European
literary experience" *(The Islands in Between* pp. 86 - 99). But, and
this brings up the second historical issue, this is precisely the
emphasis that the dominant traditions of West Indian literature
and criticism have shunned. Instead West Indian writers have
preferred to define their work with reference to what they perceive
as a distinctive West Indian experience. Indeed the West Indian
writer has been the most insistent, and certainly the most persuasive, articulator of a West Indian consciousness which defines a
special cultural identity in the region and its literature, and which
in the process endows that literature with a unifying principle and
with a corporate national image. And in so far as this consciousness
is pervasive and explicit in West Indian literature it contributes to a
distinctive ethos that may include but certainly goes beyond the
"mastery of the European literary experience." According to the
Barbadian historian and poet, Edward Brathwaite, Caribbean
culture "contains within itself a 'culture' different from, though not
exclusive of Europe. . . . In a dynamic, working sense, each
culture becomes definitive not only in itself, but in relation to
others on which it impinges. West Indian culture from this point of
view, is identifiable in relation to the culture, say, of Latin
America, of North America, of West Africa, of Western Europe;
but it also exists as West Indian in terms of its social structures, its
politics, its deposits of history."[3] Brathwaite's observations are
significant to those norms of literary criticism and cultural analysis
which he espouses here in opposition to an exclusive Western
mode. But they are even more important to the student of West Indian literature when they are considered as a primary motive, or
active principle in the imagination of writers like Edward
Brathwaite himself. In other words, an "identifiable" West Indian
experience is a conscious objective, not only for Brathwaite the
critic but also for Brathwaite the poet and other poets and
novelists. In the words of Sylvia Wynter, "I write . . . to attempt
to define what this thing is to *be*—a Jamaican, a West Indian, an
American. I believe that this definition is the beginning of
awareness."[4] Or, according to George Lamming, West Indian fiction has been a means of investigating "the inner experience of the
West Indian community," with the result that the category "West

Indian," formerly understood as "a geographical term," now assumes "cultural significance."[5]

Literature, then, allows the West Indian to perceive the past not only in terms of its brutality and waste, but also with reference to that creative sense of self-affirmation which salvages a cultural identity from that past. Writers like Lamming and Wynter emphasize this affirmative tradition in their art because, in their view, there is always the danger that the negations of the past (slavery, colonization, racism) may be accepted as the permanent absolutes of the West Indian condition. This is the kind of acceptance which appears to have inspired one of V. S. Naipaul's more notorious homilies on the West Indies: "History was built around achievement and creation and nothing was created in the West Indies."[6] Conversely, when Edward Brathwaite stresses that cultural distinctiveness which resulted from the West Indian past, he is rebutting the notion that West Indian history is "nothing"; and he is questioning the allied assumption that, having been historically denied a distinctive culture of their own, then perforce, the West Indies have no claims to a literary tradition of their own.

It is necessary to dwell at some length on the deliberate self-definitions in West Indian literature and criticism because the major trends in West Indian poetry over the last two centuries need to be examined in the light of a growing West Indian consciousness. That growth has been slow, even imperceptible at times. But the full emergence of that national consciousness since the last world war, and more recently, since independence, demands an awareness of those critical assumptions and cultural motives which have been voiced by the writers themselves, especially since these assumptions and motives are inherent in the region's literary history in general and in the evolution of the poetry in particular. Over the years the most impressive poets have been the ones whose insistent cultural consciousness is integrated with the sophisticated structures of their art. Indeed more often than not this technical sophistication is consistent with, even demanded by, the rather complex vision that is intrinsic to the West Indian "idea" described by Brathwaite and others; for that idea simultaneously encompasses the unique West Indian situation, the definitive links with the West Indian's non-Caribbean sources, the archetypal significance of the West Indian in the New World and in the human condition at large, and finally, the West Indian identity and the poetic imagination itself as symbols of the human capacity to transform the "nothingness" of the past into the source of a creative self-consciousness.

Altogether then, the history of West Indian poetry may be perceived and treated in terms of an evolving cultural consciousness which is manifest in the deliberate articulation of a West Indian identity and in the equally deliberate, though not always successful, search for distinctive forms—for a distinctive poetic language. There is more than a coincidental relationship between this latter search for form and the West Indian's poetic quest for a cultural identity. For one of the central paradoxes of West Indian literature (one that it shares to a degree with African literatures in European languages) has been the historical requirement of using the colonial language, complete with its cultural, literary, and philosophical heritage, in order to describe a West Indian experience which remains rooted in its socio-linguistic inheritance from the West, but which has increasingly insisted on its own non-Western, even anti-Western, modes of perception and self-expression. These modes are often the result of fusing English language and English literary tradition, on the one hand, with non-Western and West Indian forms or sensibilities, on the other hand. In effect, the artist's realization of a West Indian selfhood is integrated with the perfection of literary forms that must not only be polished for their own sake but are also a reflection of the complex process of self-realization which they describe. In this regard poetic language is a part of the cultural experience, and it assumes the significance which Frantz Fanon attributes to the relationship between colonials and the colonizing language: "Every colonized people . . . finds itself face to face with the language of the civilizing nation; that is, with the culture of the mother country."[7] The precise nature of the confrontation between the colonial and the metropolitan language may therefore be important to the relationship between the literature of the former and the metropolitan literature. In West Indian poetry this relationship has evolved from the derivativeness and bald imitations of the eighteenth, nineteenth, and early twentieth centuries to the deep-seated, creative ambivalence which characterizes much of major West Indian poetry. It is the kind of ambivalence which George Lamming, among others, has described in terms of the Shakespearean archetypes, Prospero and Caliban: having been "converted" (that is, "civilized") by the language of Prospero the colonizer, the rebellious Caliban-colonial uses "this gift of language" in the "transformation" of his cultural identity" (*The Pleasures of Exile,* p. 15).

It is logical and realistic enough to describe the history of West Indian poetry as a movement from the derivativeness and colonial "conversions" of the earlier years to the more imaginative and complex "transformations" of the contemporary period. And this is a major objective in the present study. But the study also attempts to avoid the impression, which seems endemic in historical surveys of any literature, that West Indian poetry has developed through neatly patterned phases, each one as separate from its predecessor as it is from its successor, and each one characterized by unique "movements" or "schools." This approach is often more significant as the historian's convenience than as historical accuracy. It is important to describe those traditions or habits which have dominated specific periods—the neoclassical imitations in the eighteenth century, the anemic pastoralism of the nineteenth and early twentieth centuries, the rise of nationalism since the 1930's, the radicalism and the intense introspectiveness of the postindependence period, and so forth. But it is also important to bear in mind that these various historical patterns are often concurrent rather than neatly consecutive. Hence while the Caribbean "Georgics" of an expatriate poet like James Grainger may accurately reflect the dominant temper of eighteenth-century West Indian poetry—what there was of it—from the historical perspective the ambiguities of the black Francis Williams make him the most significant poet of the period precisely because he does not write wholly within the expatriate's servilely neoclassical tradition. Williams' ethnic concerns are unique in the poetry of his period, but however muted, those concerns do anticipate the major developments in modern West Indian poetry. Conversely, as a host of still flourishing West Indian "Wordsworths" demonstrate in our own time, the tradition of a bald, colonial derivativeness in West Indian poetry has died hard, if at all. Consequently, although it is convenient here, from a historian's viewpoint, to describe the phases of West Indian poetry in sequence, the literature is especially resistant to this kind of treatment beyond a certain level. Like many "emerging" literatures, West Indian literature is still in the process of clarifying its own distinctiveness and of delimiting its relationships with its various sources. It not only requires a sensitivity to its evolving distinctiveness, it also demands a sense of balance in relation to the flux and change that is inherent in the evolutionary process itself.

Acknowledgments

Sections of this study have appeared in *Journal of Popular Culture* (Bowling Green University) and *World Literature Written in English* (University of Texas, Arlington), and I wish to acknowledge the kind permission of the editors to use these materials.

I also wish to acknowledge the assistance and advice of those who contributed to the preparation of this study, particularly Sir Phillip M. Sherlock (Secretary General of the Association of Caribbean Universities), Robert McDowell (Department of English, University of Texas, Arlington), Edward Baugh and Mervyn Morris (Department of English, University of the West Indies, Jamaica), Mr. Hugh Morrison (University Radio, University of the West Indies, Jamaica), Lionel Hutchinson and members of the Barbados Writers' Workshop, and the staffs of the West India Reference Library, Barbados Public Library, National Library of Guyana, and the University of the West Indies Library (Jamaica and Trinidad campuses).

Chronology

1759   Francis Williams (1700 - 1770), a free Jamaican Black, writes his "Ode to Governor Haldane," the first known poem published by a Black West Indian.

1764   James Grainger (1723 - 1767), a British doctor on a tour of duty in the British Caribbean, publishes his "Caribbean Georgic," *Sugar Cane*.

1833   Abolition of slavery in the British colonies. M. J. Chapman's *Barbados*, a poem by a pro slavery Barbadian planter.

1883   Egbert Martin (1859 - 1887), *Leo's Poetical Works*. The emergence of the first major poet in British Guiana (now known as Guyana).

1889   Birth, in Jamaica, of Claude McKay, traditionally assumed to have been born in 1890 or 1891.

1912   Claude McKay, *Songs of Jamaica* and *Constab Ballads*. First major collections of dialect poetry in the West Indies.

1919   Racial unrest in the United States. McKay's poetry wins him recognition as a major voice in black American literature, particularly during the "Harlem Renaissance" of the 1920's.

1922   The launching of Marcus Garvey's Back-to-Africa movement with the founding of the Universal Negro Improvement Association in Harlem. McKay publishes *Harlem Shadows*.

1923   Founding of the Jamaican Poetry League by John E. C. McFarlane (1894 - 1962) and others.

1929   John E. C. McFarlane edits *Voice from the Summerland*, the first major anthology of Jamaican poetry.

1930 -   The worldwide depression has repercussions throughout
1938   the British West Indies. Labor unrest sparks the emergence of modern independence movements and of nationalist themes in contemporary West Indian poetry.

1930   Una Marson (1905 - 1965) publishes *Tropic Reveries*, the first of four volumes by one of the rare women poets of note in the West Indies. Followed by *Heights and Depths* (1931), *The Moth and the Star* (1937), and *Towards the Stars* (1945).

1931   *Guianese Poetry: 1831 - 1931*, ed. Norman E. Cameron. The first major anthology of poetry in then British Guiana.

1942   Founding of the literary magazine, *Bim*, in Barbados, to be followed in 1943 by *Focus* in Jamaica and in 1945 by *Kyk-over-al* in British Guiana.

1948   Death of Claude McKay. Founding of the University of the West Indies.

1950   The increasing postwar migration of West Indians to Great Britain includes a substantial number of West Indian writers whose works are subsequently heard on the British Broadcasting Corporation's "Caribbean Voices" series.

1951   Arthur J. Seymour (born 1914) launches Miniature Poet Series for a four year period in which he published several new and established West Indian poets in pamphlet form.

1954   Martin Carter (born 1927), *Poems of Resistance;* Wilson Harris (born 1921), *Eternity to Season.*

1959   Frank Collymore (born 1893), *Collected Poems.*

1961   *Kyk-over-al* ceases publication.

1962   Derek Walcott (born 1930), *In a Green Night.* Jamaica and Trinidad gain independence, to be followed over the next decade by Barbados, Guyana (formerly British Guiana), and territories in the Leeward and Windward Islands.

1965   Derek Walcott, *The Castaway.*

1966   Louise Bennett (born 1919), *Jamaica Labrish.*

1967   Edward Brathwaite (born 1930), *Rights of Passage*, the first of a trilogy, to be followed by *Masks* (1968) and *Islands* (1969).

1969   Derek Walcott, *The Gulf.* The Black Power movement extends its influence from the United States of America to the literature and politics of the West Indies, with Black Power advocates launching an abortive revolt in Trinidad in 1970.

1972   First Caribbean Festival of the Arts (Carifesta) is held in Georgetown, Guyana, with representatives from all language areas of the Caribbean. Wayne Brown *(On the Coast)*, Anthony McNeill *(Reel from "The Life Movie")*, and Dennis Scott *(Uncle Time*, 1973) emerge as the major representatives of the young generation of post-independence poets of the 1970's.

CHAPTER 1

The Beginnings: 1760 - 1940

T HE first one hundred eighty years of West Indian poetry
are uneven at best, and in some respects are downright
unpromising. Of course the period as a whole was one in which
there was a flourishing tradition of oral poetry, in the folk songs,
spirituals and calypsoes which went back to slavery and bore the
distinct forms of African as well as Western influences, and which
have not only become increasingly important in literate poetry as
such, but are also winning recognition as crucial aspects of West
Indian poetry in their own right. But with the exception of
Jamaica's Claude McKay no major poet emerges in this early
period. The prevailing poetic tradition was one of colonial imitativeness, especially in the mode of English Romantic and early
Victorian poetry. But on the more promising side, it is possible to
detect the slow development of a socially motivated and culturally
conscious tradition which is as old as the tradition of colonial imitativeness and which reaches its fullest, most powerful expression
in the works of Claude McKay just before the emergence of the
postwar generation of writers in the 1940's. Indeed, in several of
the more interesting writers of this period both traditions are in
evidence, and in such cases the writers are rather apt representatives of their period, for it was one in which the settled attitudes
of colonial acceptance and imitativeness were increasingly being
challenged by the kind of restive questioning that later matured
into the nationalist movements, in both literature and politics.

I   *The Eighteenth Century: Pastorialism and the
Roots of National Consciousness*

James Grainger's *Sugar Cane* (1764) is the first poem written in
the West Indies to win any noticeable response from the outside
world. The occasion was less than auspicious. Grainger's pastoral

19

epic on Caribbean plantation life aroused some hilarity, but little else, in the literary circle of Samuel Johnson, Joshua Reynolds, James Boswell and their friends.[1] Their amusement is understandable. Grainger's work is a very unimaginative and absurdly pretentious attempt to create what the author calls "a West India Georgic" but which struck Johnson and others as a ludicrous imitation of Homer and Virgil. But quite apart from its intrinsic lack of merit, *Sugar Cane* is significant as an early example of what has become a long-lived tradition in West Indian poetry. It is the tradition of the Caribbean pastoral, written by British expatriates like Grainger, a Scottish doctor of medicine, or in later generations by local West Indians of all backgrounds. It is based on the unimaginative imitation of popular literary forms in Western Europe, ranging from the epic and picturesque modes of the eighteenth century, to the nature poetry of the nineteenth-century British Romantics. Like countless expatriate and locally born poets since his time Grainger perceives the West Indies as mere landscape, an exotic landscape rich in "picturesque" images. In keeping with his superficially pastoral mode he can see the plantation only as a species of Utopia, with its slaves as happy swains, "all-jocund, o'er the long-hoed land." Grainger is not entirely indifferent to the moral implications of slavery. There is a passing wish that slavery might eventually give way to laws which will replace black slaves with black "servants" who will continue to cultivate the cane—by "choice." This limited perception, or nonperception, of black humanity is typical of the genre that Grainger pioneers in *Sugar Cane*. The Caribbean pastoral has always extolled the beauties of the West Indian landscape to the exclusion of any perceived West Indian experience, or at the most, in conjunction with a patronizing and selfindulgent view of the folk as exotic swains and "servants of choice." The severely limited moral vision complements the shallow derivativeness with which the poet handles his borrowed forms.

On the other hand Grainger's period also witnessed the beginning of a more far-reaching tradition with the work of Francis Williams, a free Jamaican black. Unfortunately most of our knowledge of Williams is derived from Edward Long's racially distorted *History of Jamaica* (1774). As far as can be determined Williams was educated in England through the patronage of the Duke of Montague as part of the latter's project to prove that blacks who received an education equal to that of whites could hold their own in "civilized" society. On his return to Jamaica Williams discovered that his "equal" education could not open doors to equal opportunities in a slave-owning society, and eventually opened a school as a livelihood. As a member of the white plantation class Long is openly hostile to Williams whom he describes as an upstart educated black; and this is the basis on which he handles Williams' Latin "Ode to George Haldane" in honor of a new colonial governor. But neither Long's inept translation nor his prejudices as critic really obscure the fact that Williams' ode is the first poem on record which voices, albeit covertly, the duality of the West Indian as the despised and uprooted African ("Aethiop") and as the dispossessed heir of the West. And in exploring this duality the poet voices that sense of a peculiarly West Indian "belonging" which transcends the history of dispossession and which has become an enduring hallmark of ethnocultural themes in West Indian poetry: "In this prolific isle I drew my birth, / And *Britain* nurs'd, illustrious throughout the earth, / This, my lov'd isle."

The accompanying racial protest is handled with the covert but deft irony for which his black American contemporary, Phillis Wheatley, is only now beginning to receive belated credit. The formal flattery of the ode is skillfully manipulated by a talent that obviously knows how to adapt established forms for its own innovative statement. Hence the expected flattery of his subject depends in part on a racial self-depreciation that echoes the usual white slurs. But his self-depreciation is edged with irony in the poet's pointed reminder that all humanity shares "one common soul," irrespective of race:

> This rule was 'stablish'd by th' Eternal Mind;
> Nor virtue's self, nor prudence are confin'd
> To *colour;* none imbues the honest heart;
> To science none belongs, and none to art.

And, anticipating a later generation of West Indian "Calibans," Williams links the satire of covert racial protest with a self-conscious emphasis on the duality of his language and art. The despised African has assumed the "learned speech" of his detractors in order to proclaim his humanity and to assert his sense of belonging to his island:

Manners unsullied, and the radiant glow
Of genius, burning with desire to *know;*
And learned speech, with modest accent worn,
Shall best the sooty *African* adorn.[2]

Grainger and Williams produced the only significant West Indian poetry to survive from that period. Although writers like John
Wolcot (Peter Pindar) had temporary personal links with the area,
their work has nothing to do with the West Indies. Neither did
they claim otherwise. But taken together, Grainger and Williams
demonstrate that two of the dominant traditions of West Indian
poetry have their roots in the middle of the eighteenth century.
Grainger's expatriate pastoral anticipates the derivative landscape
painting which reached its heyday at the turn of the twentieth century and which still flourishes. Moreover his own explanation of his
interest in the West Indian landscape (the Caribbean is a ready-
made source of picturesque images) has lasting implications for the
tradition which he helped to establish. The peculiar beauties of the
Caribbean offer an open invitation to the landscape painter, especially to the versifier who has little else to say. Of course
landscape painting as such is not peculiar to West Indian literature.
But as Grainger and others were to develop it, the Caribbean
pastoral reflects the intellectual and cultural relationship between
the colonial West Indian's writing and its European sources.
Motivated wholly by the desire to imitate the European model,
Sugar Cane and its successors within the tradition are predictably
derivative: the colonial need to mimic the mother country is
reflected in a slavish imitation of the European pastoral mode. On
the other hand, Williams' very brief output has far-reaching
significance, because he so clearly moves beyond the act of merely
borrowing the European's forms. His is the earliest recorded voice
of the West Indian attempting to define his simultaneous
relationships with old, non-Western roots, and with a new world in
which he is both an heir and an outcast. His ethnic self-perception
and his vision of *his* isle are therefore pointing the direction in
which the mainstream of West Indian poetry is to flow.

II   *The Nineteenth Century: The Challenge to the Colonial Tradition*

The historical significance of Grainger and Williams is limited to
the degree to which they represent their respective traditions. As

individual artists their achievements are limited. Apart from Williams' talent for covert satire their poetry is mediocre at best, and in this regard their work anticipates the uniform mediocrity of West Indian poetry in the nineteenth century. As has already been pointed out, the nineteenth century is the heyday of a Caribbean pastoral in which hackneyed nature verse in the Romantic mode alternates with the colonial's embarrassingly sycophantic verses in praise of the British Empire. In this regard M.J. Chapman's *Barbadoes* (1833) is an indisputable heir to Grainger's *Sugar Cane*. Chapman is the self-conscious contributor to a Caribbean pastoral tradition. And this fact, together with his anti-abolitionist prejudices, ensure that *Barbadoes* remains a bland collection of pastoral clichés on the Barbadian landscape, interspersed here and there with the usual images of happy black slaves. On the whole the writers of Guyana (then British Guiana) are the most widely known and most accessible of the earlier half of the century, due largely to N.E. Cameron's 1931 anthology.[3] But it is doubtful that most of Cameron's nineteenth-century writers are of any importance to anyone except the literary antiquarian. Among the more notable entries there is Henry G. Dalton who is credited with being the first poet to deal with local Guyanese subjects. On the basis of a work like "Essequibo and its Tributaries" there is no doubt that Dalton is fascinated, as later, more competent writers were to be, with the awesome sense of power and space that is inspired by the continental dimensions of Guyana's South American landscape. But as references to savages and "niggers" attest, nothing can really be expected from Dalton by way of a complex vision of a Guyanese experience. (*Guianese Poetry* pp. 25 - 43).

Egbert Martin ("Leo") is the most distinguished poet of the period in Guyana and the West Indies as a whole. But that distinction reflects the generally lackluster performance of his contemporaries rather than any really superior merit in Martin himself. Like his contemporaries, Martin writes firmly within the tradition of the Caribbean pastoral, in imitation of the English Romantics. This imitativeness is particularly strong in his *Poetical Works*. The standard God-in-Nature theme informs poems like "Moonrise" and "Sky Pictures," and these are as poorly written as the banal, stock-in-trade nature verses of "Sorrel Tree" and "The Wren." This sensitivity to the English Romantic mode is matched, in the true tradition of the Caribbean pastoral, by the colonial's loyalty to the Empire. Such loyalty is not without its rewards. "Verses Written for the National Anthem" was awarded the first prize in a London newspaper competition in honor of Queen Victoria's Jubilee. Like the earlier "Welcome" which was written to greet the visiting Prince of Wales, "Verses" celebrates Britain's right to spread her wings "O'er her colonial throng;" and in the classical colonial situation the Guyanese-born Martin is as fiercely English as his British expatriate counterparts. "Welcome" is the black Englishman's self-congratulation on being a "living branch . . . from the parent tree . . . loyal and free" (*Guianese Poetry*, pp 107-108).

But to his credit, Martin's work is not limited to banal naturescapes and colonial posturings. His better works are those in which he looks at the human condition with specific reference to the disadvantages of the impoverished folk. The long narrative poem "Ruth" in *Poetical Works* is an unevenly written but generally compassionate story of rural poverty. It is the tragedy of a young man who dies in a search for gold in Venezuela, and whose death triggers that of his young heartbroken wife. On the evidence of works like "Ruth," Martin is at his best in a narrative form and in the evocative description of people, particularly the description of the poor and the oppressed. The description of the Amerindian's tragic decay in "Hammock Maker" is another example of that talent. And the ethnic sympathies which are a motive in the portrayal of the dispossessed Indian are clearly in evidence in "The Negro Village." This work evinces a racial pride and a strong indignation at historical injustices to blacks, and on both counts is comparable with that of a Guyanese contemporary, T. R. F. Elliot whose "Emancipation Chorus" is included in Cameron's anthology (*Guianese Poetry* p. 42).

None of the religious homilies in a later collection, *Lyrics*, matches the modest achievement of the ethnosocial narratives of *Poetical Works*. On the whole that achievement reflects a significant duality in Martin. The hackneyed nature verses and the songs of Empire hark back to, and celebrate, the black colonial's ingrained loyalties to the mother culture. But at the same time, the poems about the black, the Indian, and the poor represent a major breakthrough in nineteenth-century West Indian poetry. This aspect of Martin's work is the first substantial body of poetry that promises to break away from the long strangle hold of a stultifying colonial imitativeness, In these works the poet is attempting to look with both originality and compassion at his human environment.

However, these two aspects of Martin's work are not a mere contradiction. Instead, taken together they represent the double-consciousness of an emerging poetic tradition which is still rooted in strongly entrenched loyalties to the literary forms and imperial sovereignty of England, but which is simultaneously beginning to respond to the growing social and ethnic pressures of the late nineteenth century and early twentieth century. In this respect Martin's real significance lies in the fact that his work and the double-consciousness which it represents on a whole establish him as a watershed figure in the history of West Indian poetry. He harks back to the older traditions which still survive, even in post-colonial West Indian literature, but which are already being challenged in his own works by a new, less complacent sense of race and history. If the ties with James Grainger and his kind are often obvious, so too are the ties with the covert ethnicity of Francis Williams and with the emerging nationalism of the twentieth century.

III   *1900 - 1940: From Pastoralism to Social Protest and Cultural Nationalism*

Of more immediate significance, Martin's poetry makes him the forerunner of that period of transition which characterizes the first forty years of the present century. These are years in which the old Caribbean pastoral continues to flourish. W. A. Roberts' *Pan and Peacock*, for example, lives up to its title in that it is as self-consciously Neoclassical in its pastoral themes as anything that appeared during James Grainger's period. Despite his Jamaican background Roberts is closer to the spirit of the Scotsman, William Morrison, whose Jamaican-based *Poems* is largely a collection of tritely patriotic hymns addressed to the mother country. But the pastoral tradition exits side by side with a heightened *local* self-consciousness regarding national identity and the role of the artist. On the one hand, the founding of the Jamaican Poetry League, as an extension of the Empire Poetry League, attests to the strength of imperial loyalties. But on the other hand, it reflects the sense of some local literary identity or movement which merges in the 1930's and 1940's with the political movements for independence throughout the Caribbean. This nascent nationalism is implicit in the very appearance of general anthologies by John E. C. McFarlane in Jamaica and by Cameron in Guyana. It also informs even the substandard landscape poetry of the more forgettable

writers of the period. Constance Hollar, a member of the Jamaican
Poetry League, is one such writer. Her collection, *Flaming June*,
published in 1941, actually brings together poems that had been
written and published separately since 1915. It attests to the perennial popularity of Jamaican flora among aspiring Jamaican poets,
but the prevailing mediocrity is relieved from time to time by the
enthusiastic celebration of a Jamaican *presence* in her landscape.
This is also true of Vivian Virtue, a fellow league member, whose
work enjoys a popularity with Jamaican anthologists that is hardly
justified by its calibre. Altogether, in this nondescript body of
poetry the Caribbean pastoral remains as insipidly escapist as it has
ever been, but occasionally some of the writers in the pastoral
tradition do manage to emphasize its Caribbean context in a way
that anticipates the more fully developed cultural nationalism of
the major twentieth-century writers.

This tentative national consciousness is not limited to the more
readable pastoral writers of the turn of the century. Vere T. Daly's
"Song of Young Guiana," for example, is a baldly anticolonial
statement, but despite the unimaginative writing it is a significant
precursor of that intensely defiant nationalism which was to
characterize Guyanese poetry during the pre-independence period
of the 1950's and 1960's: "It is better by far to be wild, free men
than the scopeless / And prince-governed men of tears."(*Guianese
Poetry* pp. 111 - 112). One of Daly's more substantial contemporaries, Walter M. Lawrence, shares this intensity. "Forward
Guiana's Sons" (*Guianese Poetry*, p. 179) is a spirited call for
national purpose that is repeated throughout the posthumous *The
Poet of Guiana*. Accordingly, "Guiana: Allegory" voices outrage at
the indignities of the colonial experience. The anticolonial theme is
rooted in the intense feelings that have become a hallmark of
Guyanese protest poetry, and it is combined with a passionate sense
of a common humanity in another work, "Guiana":

> The years—lost years that the rest of the world had
>   filled with the treasures of Time,
> Have bequeathed thee nought but a name that to claim,
>   were just a magnificent crime,—
> Have left thee less than the dust of decay piled up to
>   Imperial shame;
> And the light that lighteth Ambition's rough road has
>   paled to a flickering flame.

> But Hope, high up the tenebrious sky, o'ershines the
> inglorious Night
> And a cry goes up (and the voice is the voice that
> speaketh of impotent might)
> From gods, not men.—what a people are here! Guiana,
> they're hoping again,
> For the cry goes up from the deepest despair; God gives us
> a chance to be men![4]

In spite of occasional pretentiousness ("tenebrious sky") and clichés ("flickering flame") this is a fairly effective piece of writing which easily places Lawrence above many of his contemporaries. There are signs of a carefully controlled sense of the dramatic that moves from the somber repetitions of the early statements ("Have bequeathed . . . Have left. . . .") to the passionate cry of despair and defiance. Lawrence's forte lies in the intensity that convinces his reader of his sincerity. But his achievement also rests on the ability to evoke multiple responses to his language. Hence the cry on behalf of a national destiny is also a plea on behalf of all human beings yearning to realize their humanity to its fullest. The colonial ambition to be free and to be achievers is a microcosm of the human spirit's need to fulfill its potential. It is this kind of potential that allows the poet to perceive human beings as "gods" in that they participate in the creation and growth of their own humanity. Their cry against the deadening impact of colonialism is therefore both a specifically Guyanese self-affirmation and a part of humanity's general quest for self-realization at all costs.

Lawrence's emphasis on the *universal* significance of his national theme has important implications for the subsequent development of national consciousness in West Indian poetry as a whole. For this is the kind of emphasis which rejects a popular image of universality as something which somehow transcends, even exists apart from, individual and national, or ethnic, consciousness. The quest for an individual identity and for the distinctive contours of one's personality is not antithetical to the experience of a universal humanity. Indeed it is one of the most universal of human experiences; and by a similar token, so is the search for an ethnic identity and a national consciousness. Consequently, for Lawrence and West Indian poets since then the West Indian experience not only has its identifiable distinctiveness, but it corresponds with and is actually a microcosm of the universal quest for individual purpose and moral

order. In this respect there is a marked similarity between
Lawrence's national themes and the work of more recent poets like
Derek Walcott. But unlike his major successors in the generation of
writers who follow him, Lawrence is still constrained to counter-
balance his anticolonial themes with the pervasive imperial
loyalties of the early twentieth century—particularly on the death
of George V ("Royal Requiem") and the ascension of George VI
("Coronation Ode"). Neither is he any more successful than most
of his contemporaries in avoiding the cloying excesses of the Caribbean pastoral. P. H. Daly, the editor of his selected poems, actually
praises "Kaieteur" as "precisely what a Swinburnian ode should
be, a glittering necklace of work diamonds." And in the shorter
landscape poem "Call of the Wild" the influence of Wordsworth is
suffocating. But notwithstanding Daly's enthusiasm for the imitations of Swinburne's work, the truth is that Lawrence fails to
develop his undeniable potential because he devoted so much of
his talent to churning out replicas of Wordsworth and Swinburne.
For example, "Kaieteur" shows flashes of the intense feeling that is
the main strength of "Guiana," but on the whole it is merely a
mechanical imitation of Swinburne. On balance, however, his
much abused potential makes him an apt representative of the
achievements and failures of his generation. Like their more accomplished nineteenth-century predecessors they combine an underdeveloped but promising vision of a West Indian destiny with a
slavish loyalty to the literary heritage and political hegemony of the
British Empire. On this basis Lawrence is comparable with his
more noteworthy contemporaries in what is generally a decidedly
undistinguished period of West Indian poetry, other notables being
Thomas MacDermot, John E. C. McFarlane, and Una Marson
(Claude McKay, whose achievements place him well above
everyone else in this period, will be dealt with in a separate
chapter).

Of these three, MacDermot and McFarlane have enjoyed a certain prestige, particularly during the 1920's and 1930's. MacDermot was posthumously declared Jamaica's first poet laureate
(1910 -1933). And even as late as the 1950's a major public library
in the island was named after him. On the whole, however, there is
no evidence in the works of either MacDermot or McFarlane that
would justify this prestige on literary merit as such. MacDermot
was born in Jamaica in 1870 of Irish parents, and eventually moved
permanently to England for reasons of ill-health. In view of this

personal background it is not surprising that he contributes generously to the sentimental excesses of the Caribbean pastoral. The usual, idyllic images of the Jamaican landscape are liberally coated with the exile's nostalgia and are trotted out in the baldly derivative style of the genre. MacDermot's popularity in his lifetime and some time thereafter rests in that strong affection for Jamaica which permeates his main collections of poetry, *Orange Valley and other Poems* and *Brown's Town Ballads and other Poems*. In "The Brown Mountain Village," for example, the exile's nostalgia heightens the memory of Jamaica as a mother image, as the source of the poet's immediate sense of identity.[5] And "Orange Valley," the title poem of the same collection, demonstrates his strong sense of a Jamaican history which touches upon his concept of a Jamaican identity (*Orange Valley*, pp. 21 - 23). Of course this affection for a mother Jamaica must be seen in the larger context of his overriding loyalty to England, *the* mother country. The occasional anticolonial wrath of the Guyanese Lawrence is quite alien to MacDermot's settled, unruffled temperament, and there is nothing in his work to suggest that he is capable even of Lawrence's fitful anti-imperialism. Consequently the poems about Jamaica are often the usual mechanical hymns in the mode of "My Beautiful Home" (*Orange Valley*, p. 1).

MacDermot's limitations as a craftsman are matched by the shallowness of his poetic vision. The trite language of poems like "My Beautiful Home" seems perversely appropriate in the long run because although there is no reason to doubt his affections for his island, he demonstrates no capacity to transform those feelings into a coherent and complex vision of his society and experience. Instead the *Orange Valley* collection offers the shallow word-painting of "Now the Lignum Vitae Blows" and "On the First of May." Moreover, given his British sensibilities and the remoteness of the white Jamaican from the lives of most Jamaicans there is always the danger that this kind of shallowness will easily lend itself to a distortive image of the Jamaican experience. "Jamaica's August Hymn," written to celebrate the anniversary of the abolition of slavery, presents such an image, based in this instance on the white, upperclass Jamaican's cherished myth of a multiracial, harmonious society: "Class and race united stand / Equal laws and equal favour, / Rule through all our happy land" (*Orange Valley*, p. 24). This is not only trite and sententious as poetry but it is also a palpably false vision of MacDermot's Jamaica. But it is also the stuff of which popular verse was made in his time; it voices those guilty self-assurances with which McDermot's white and light-skinned compatriots viewed race and class in their society. Hence "Jamaica Market," by Agnes Maxwell-Hall, a contemporary of MacDermot could easily have been written by MacDermot himself: "Black skins, babel—and the sun / . . . burns all colours into one."[6] However absurd MacDermot's prestige as poet may now seem in retrospect, his popularity is a significant reflection on his cultural environment. His readership was admittedly small but then West Indians have never been famous as readers of literature, especially their own literature. But he was popular within an influential though numerically small circle of the educated elite. His limited vision of his world reflects prevailing myths, particularly about race and class, which have survived as a persistent kind of upperclass folklore in the speeches of colonial governors, their post-colonial successors, and in the usual blandishments of the tourist industry.

In view of this inability to comprehend the total Jamaican reality MacDermot's interest in the black folk strikes a false, or at best an unconvincing note. "The Mothers of the City" is a very bad poem because the flaccid language reinforces the impression that the feeling is contrived and that the poet's limited imagination cannot bridge the enormous gap between his world and the lives of Jamaica's black poor:

> Oh, who are the weary pilgrims
>   That caravan now on the way?
> 'Tis the women with market burdens
>   And their hampered donkeys gray. (*Orange Valley*, pp. 26 - 27)

It is clear enough that in this kind of poem the Jamaican poet is the heir to the pastoral tradition of James Grainger. These market women are the idealized folk of the pastoral landscape. For notwithstanding the urban reference of his title, MacDermot is really using his market women as a rural point of reference: they "Pour forth for the City's hunger / The milk from the Country's breast." Neither is McDermot any more convincing when he attempts to bridge the gap between himself and the folk by using the folk idiom, as he tries to do in "A Market Basket in the Car":

> Because you Mudda see duppy
> So put whitey wash in you 'kin
> Seems as you tink you is Buckra;
> You nayga man—ugly no sin (*Orange Valley*, p. 28

The rhyme scheme is awkwardly devised. It is a patronizing attempt to use the folk dialect in poetry by first making it more "poetic." To his credit MacDermot did recognize some possibilities in the folk idiom which his contemporary Claude McKay explored with much greater success, and at which Louise Bennett has excelled without peer in the modern period. But MacDermot is severely handicapped not only by his individual shortcomings as a poet but also by his social distance from his subject. On the whole, "A Market Basket in the Car" has very little to say, because apart from hearing and attempting to reproduce folk language the poet could say little or nothing about these people or on their behalf. And in the final analysis he can tell his readers nothing about market women except as (verbally) colorful accessories that link the city with his perennially pastoral, eternally idyllic countryside.

On the whole it is easy to understand the gusto with which West Indian anthologists have avoided MacDermot's work in recent collections of West Indian poetry. But quite apart from his severe limitations as a poet MacDermot's work remains significant in a symbolic and representative sense. It voices a vision of Jamaican society which is narrow but which continues to run deep in some circles. It is a vision which has been no less long-lived for being limited in scope. After all the pastoral's unchanging rural setting both symbolizes and encourages a sense of idyllic stasis, especially for those whose life-styles are threatened by changes in the real world. In fact the enduring significance of MacDermot's circle and of its vision is really underscored by the passionate energies with which the younger, politically motivated writers of our own time address not only Jamaican but West Indian society as a whole.

The posthumous award of laureateship to MacDermot in 1933 was largely the work of the Jamaican Poetry League, founded ten years previously by John E. Clare McFarlane. Unlike MacDermot, McFarlane was of black Jamaican parentage, but his education and social background (he was a civil servant) placed him within the intellectual establishment. He is a more prolific writer than MacDermot with three long narrative poems and two collections of shorter

poems to his credit. He also published over a longer period, from
the turn of the century into the 1950's. But on the whole his poetry
is no more substantial than MacDermot's. The narrative poems are
all pedestrian at best; at their worst they are heavy-handedly
moralistic and embarrassingly derivative. The full title of the first
one is ominous enough: *Beatrice: Narrative Poem in Ten Parts in
Classical Metre*. The narrative itself is a pastoral love story that
manages, somehow, to combine the styles of eighteenth-century
sentimental tragedy and nineteenth-century melodrama. *Daphne* is
another pastoral tale, about star-crossed lovers; and as in the earlier
work, the Jamaican setting is largely incidental, except as the stylized pastoral background. The third narrative poem, *Magdalen:
The Story of Supreme Love* exploits Biblical sources for much of
the unimaginative didacticism that marks his later works. *Selected
Shorter Poems* offers the familiar range of unimaginative and poorly executed themes: the romanticized landscape ("Hope River").
the praises of Empire ("All Things Await Thee") coexisting with a
limited Jamaican consciousness ("My Country"), "The Black Peril"
is an unusual poem for McFarlane in that it is preoccupied with
racial identity and black pride: it offers a vigorous defence of
Ethiopia and blacks in general against racial slurs by a British
magazine writer in 1923. But that is the extent of McFarlane's
ethnic themes. On the whole his achievements as a poet are
minimal. His more important contribution lies in his personal work
in helping to promote the idea of a Jamaican poetic tradition, an
idea that is perhaps the real saving grace of the Jamaican Poetry
League and of McFarlane's poetry.

Una Marson's poetry has not received even the understandably
limited attention that has been given to MacDermot and
McFarlane. But on the whole her poetry is considerably more substantial than that of her two older contemporaries. Of her four
collections of poems the first, *Tropic Reveries*, is extremely immature. It is a combination of adolescent love lyrics and the standard nature verses. But in the next two collections, *Heights and
Depths* and *The Moth and the Star*, she matures rapidly, becoming
the most ambitious Jamaican poet of the early 1930's, with the exception of Claude McKay. (Her fourth volume, *Towards the Stars*,
is largely a reprint of poems from the second and third).[7] She is the
earliest female poet of significance to emerge in West Indian
literature. This is important in itself because she was not merely a
woman who happened to write poetry, but a female poet whose

works were concerned, to a considerable degree, with the situation
and identity of the West Indian woman. In Marson's work the sexual perspectives of the woman are integrated with the cultural and
racial themes which she clearly shares with Claude McKay. Louise
Bennett is the only other woman in Jamaican and West Indian
literature with comparable or superior achievements to her credit
in this regard.

Heights and Depths is a transitional collection. It continues some
of the immaturities of *Tropic Reveries*. The obligatory landscape
painting is as trite as usual, but at the same time she is beginning
to explore the ethnosexual themes which are to dominate her later
work. "In Jamaica" voices a sense of belonging and racial solidarity, but it suffers from a flabby style in which the usual clichés
about the "exotic" tropics and smiling "darkies" attest to Marson's
lingering attachment to the alien perspectives of the Caribbean
pastoral. She is on surer ground in "There Will Come a Time"
where she is interested not in the outsider's fantasies about the
tropics, but in the real experience of the black West Indian:

> We who see through the hypocrisy . . .
> . . . . feel the blood of black and white alike
> Course through our veins as our strong heritage
> Must range ourselves to build the younger race.
>
> (*Heights and Depths*, p. 45)

The poem is technically uneven, relying at times on an overly
preachy directness. But at other times that directness takes the
form of a colloquial straightforwardness which contrasts refreshingly with the stylized clichés of her earlier works, and which
represents an emotional power and honesty. Indeed that emotional
power accounts for much of the vibrancy and the generally relaxed
tone which mark the less pedestrian areas of her style. At such
points the poet's choice of themes dealing in an innovative way
with immediate experience is complemented by a vigorous
originality in expression.

"Moonlight Reverie" is a thematically promising, though
technically uneven, introduction to Marson's womanhood themes.
The poem is a sharp slap at entrenched male self-complacency.
The woman is the martyred partner of philandering husbands and
insensitive lovers, and she is equally the long-suffering mother:
"How many women at this very hour / Are filled with anxious

thoughts, and deeply pray / That lover, husband, child may mend his way" (*Heights and Depths*, p. 20). The style is uninspired, but altogether the poem sounds a relatively new note in West Indian poetry. For the first time the voice of the West Indian woman can be heard, not merely mouthing the stock banalities about the Caribbean landscape, but actually describing the experience of the woman herself.

The Moth and the Star fulfills much of the promise of the preceding volume. The racial themes have been enlarged and have been integrated with her sexual themes. The resulting enrichment, even complexity, of some themes is complemented by some stylistic innovations, notably her experimentation with the rural folk dialect in her exploration of the racial and sexual experiences of the folk. This volume also reflects Marson's maturity after migrating to England in 1932. While in England she served as secretary to the League of Colored Peoples and was private secretary to the late Emperor Haile Selassie when the Italian invasion of Ethiopia forced him into exile in the United Kingdom. At this phase of her development as a writer Marson is comparable with Claude McKay in so far as exile to a predominantly white society sharpens her ethnic perception. In this regard their experiences anticipate a major aspect of West Indian literature in general, especially since the Second World War: exile from the West Indies inspires and heightens racial perception and cultural consciousness; from the distance of cold, bleak England the memories of the West Indies intensify feelings of (black) racial solidarity and a West Indian consciousness.

But in addition to all of this Marson's exile-as-perception is interwoven with a persistent awareness of her sexual identity and its implications for her racial experience. Hence "Little Brown Girl" does not merely record the impressions of a brown-skinned Jamaican in the homogenous whiteness of the London winter and English faces: "White, white, white / And they seem all the same / As they say that Negroes seem" (*The Moth and the Star*, pp. 11 - 13). As the poem's title suggests, the work also explores the young girl's insecurity and vulnerability in this alien world, both as a West Indian stranger and as a female. In poems like these Marson's work achieves a new level of sophistication, blending racial, sexual and cultural experiences, and venturing into a much more self-confident and innovative use of language. The judicious repetitiveness ("White, white, white . . . they seem . . . they

say . . .") mimics the excited breathiness of the newcomer who is
awed by her new environment while being still able to perceive it
with a kind of malicious enthusiasm. The repetitions therefore reinforce the ethno-cultural shock of her first encounter with a ubiquitous white majority; and that shock is complemented by the
reader's surprise at the sudden, and slyly subversive reversal of
roles: it is the West Indian newcomer to England, rather than the
British visitor to the West Indies, who is now claiming that the
others all "seem the same."

That final detail exemplifies the kind of ironic penetration which
broadens her racial themes from bare protest to complex perception. "He Called Us Brethren!" takes an impish delight in the fact
that English newspapers actually think it newsworthy when a white
pastor salutes blacks as "brethren." "The Stranger" offers another
example of Marson's penchant for role reversal, a satiric technique
at which she excels. The Englishman who listens to her description
of Jamaica becomes the wistful-faced stranger rather than the host
in his own country. Her island-home now represents a vibrant
humanity, a colorful vitality to which the reserved, winter-besieged
British are strangers. Conversely, "Isolation" looks back to a time
when the British were, literally, aliens in a strange Caribbean. In
effect, the poem emphasizes the disorientation of Marson and her
fellow-migrants in England by recapturing the loneliness and the
weariness of the white colonist in the "mad tropic land" (*The Moth
and the Star*, p. 23). "Quashie Comes to London" continues the
technique of role reversal (Quashie is the black visitor reacting to
the "mad" British); but the technique also allows Marson to project images of racial self-acceptance by way of Quashie's frank
preference for black women and his Jamaican homeland, as well as
by way of his irreverent, ebullient folk dialect. The language of
"Black Fancy" returns to standard English, but with a decidedly
colloquial tone that underlines the vibrant self-confidence of the
black woman's affirmation of her racial and sexual identity, in
much the same way that the language and style of Quashie reinforces his subversive vitality:

> There is something about me
> That has a dash in it
> Especially when I put on
> My bandana. (*The Moth and the Star*, pp. 75 - 76)

In "Cinema Eyes" the simple declarative style of the first-person narrative heightens the theme of a destructive self-hatred in the black woman's experience: "I grew up with a cinema mind / . . . . I saw no beauty in black faces," the older woman remarks to her daughter in her attack on the impact of the white cinema on the black woman's sexual self-esteem. The declarative style concludes the poem on a note of quite determination which is underlined by a deft shift to shorter statements: "I will let you go / When black beauties / Are chosen for the screen" (*The Moth and the Star*, pp. 87 - 88).

The variety of styles with which Marson handles her ethnosexual themes suggests a self-confidence which has obviously increased with her maturity. Her effective variation of forms within standard English and the satiric use of dialect in "Quashie Comes to London" attest to her versatility in the development of her style. Dialect poems like "Quashie Comes to London" are relatively few in her collected works, and it is difficult to determine whether she is capable of McKay's passionate intensity in the medium, or of Louise Bennett's tremendous range of feeling and tone. But the dialect poems which do appear are clearly superior to the limited experiments of MacDermot's poetry.

As further proof of Marson's versality there is a distinct group of dialect poems in which she attempts to combine Jamaica's rural folk language with the black American's blues tradition. "Brown Baby Blues" is a corrosive satire on the black woman's racial and sexual self-hatred, presented through a mother's lullaby to her half-white baby; in "Canefield Blues" a cane-cutter moans the death of his woman and the hardships of the rural poor; and in "Kinky Hair Blues" the black woman's decision to straighten her hair is both a doleful summary of her ethnosexual insecurity and an indictment of the black man's sexual preference for nonblack standards of sexual beauty. Throughout these poems the distinctively personal statement of the blues style emphasizes the private participation in widespread ethnosexual conflicts in the black experience; but the accompanying Jamaican dialect also locates those conflicts, unequivocably, in Marson's own society. This is especially true of the blues lament in "Kinky Hair Blues":

> Gwine find a beauty shop
> Cause I ain't a belle
> The boys pass me by

> They says I's not so swell. . . .
> I like me black face
> And me kinky hair
> I like me black face
> And me kinky hair
> But nobody loves dem
> I jes don't think it's fair. (*The Moth and the Star*, p. 91)

Dialect poems of this sort are uneven. The heavier rhythms of the blues form do not harmonize well with the rapid cut-and-thrust of the Jamaican folk mood and folk style. What does salvage the poem is the complex awareness which controls its tone and overall structure. Instead of a simple straightforward complaint, the protest takes the dual form of moral indignation (at the black man and the white world) and an unsparing awareness of the speaker's complicity in her own sexual humiliation. The juxtaposition of motives complements the synthesis, albeit an unsuccessful one, of Jamaican folk idiom (with its satiric function) and black American blues (with its inherently personal self-revelation of the speaker's guilt).

These patterns of juxtaposition and synthesis point up the extent to which Marson's artistic growth takes the form of an increasing complexity of vision and form. Both the successful and the uneven variations of style and structure are a far cry from the inherited clichés of her first volume. They bring her closer to the temper and interests of the succeeding generation of postwar poets: the heightened ethnic awareness of the West Indian condition as one of exile, an increasing response to the experiences of the black American, and a willingness to adopt and experiment with both standard English and the rich resources of local dialects. Her ethnic themes reflect the cultural impact of the Harlem Renaissance of the 1920's—the blues poems, for example, are comparable with the folk poetry of America's Sterling Brown and the young Langston Hughes. But these themes also touch upon issues which would culminate in the political unrest and nationalist movements of the late 1930's and during the 1940's. If Guyana's Egbert Martin embodies the split loyalties of West Indian poetry at the turn of the century, Marson's work as a whole represents a movement from one era to the next. She moves from the clichés and stasis of the pastoral tradition to an innovative exploration of her experience; and she undertakes that exploration in terms that are sophisticated

enough to integrate political protest into a fairly complex and committed art. In her generation her achievement is surpassed only by
Claude McKay.

CHAPTER 2

The Contribution of Claude McKay

I N 1919 during a series of bloody race riots in the United
 States, Senator Henry Cabot Lodge, Sr., entered into the
Congressional Record a poem which he cited as a dangerous example of "Negro extremism." The poem was "If We Must Die," and
its publication marked the emergence of its author, Claude McKay,
as a major literary figure in black America. In turn, McKay's impact on his American contemporaries made him the first West Indian poet to achieve a significant international reputation. That
reputation has rested in part on a variety of ethnopolitical reactions
to his work, ranging from Lodge's fearful conservative outrage,
Max Eastman's quaint liberal eulogy to "the first great lyric genius
that [McKay's] race produced," and more recently, to Addison
Gayle's Black Nationalist's salute to the black "poet-warrior."[1] But
McKay's achievement as the first major West Indian poet goes
beyond the fact that he has won an international reputation for
racial protest in black America. He is of special significance in the
history of West Indian poetry because his work represents the first
sustained attempts to utilize local idioms as well as inherited European forms. And his major contribution to West Indian poetry lies
in the manner in which he succeeds as none had before him, in
describing a distinctive cultural heritage and identity, the kind of
description which has become the central focus of modern West Indian poetry.

I   *The Biographical Roots of McKay's Poetry*

McKay's personal life is bound up with the major phases of his
development as a poet. As the son of a small farmer in the Clarendon hills of Jamaica he grew up in that black rural society which
supplied him with the materials and black folk idiom which
dominate his first collections of poetry, *Songs of Jamaica* and
Constab Ballads.[2] Both collections were published in 1912 after he

left the countryside for a career as wheelwright, then as a police constable, in the city. The publication of these works was due in part to the encouragement of Walter Jekyll, an Englishman whose strong interest in McKay's dialect poetry was undoubtedly linked with his own knowledge of Jamaican folklore. While *Songs of Jamaica* is largely based on McKay's rural Jamaica, *Constab Ballads* arises from his experience in the city (Spanish Town and Kingston) as a police constable. The second volume sounds those notes of nostalgia for the rural past which are to echo throughout his later poetry; but it also voices his indignation at the brutality of urban poverty and the inequities of the social order as a whole, the kind of indignation which marks the protest poetry of the North American period. However, contrary to a prevailing and popular misconception, the first collection of poems evinces an equally painful awareness of poverty and inequities in rural Jamaica. At the same time McKay's eventual disillusionment with the city and with the constabulary was to have a lasting effect on his career since it prompted him to look elsewhere, beyond Jamaica, for a future. His personal exile took him to the United States as a student at the Tuskegee Institute, then as an odd-jobber, before he settled in New York City.

As a Jamaican McKay was no stranger to racial injustice as such—his early poems about Jamaica make that abundantly clear. But the decidedly violent realities of racial conflict in the United States were a new experience for him. The shock of this encounter sparked the intensity of the protest poems which were written in the United States. Apart from an extended visit to Russia, Western Europe, and North Africa during the 1920's McKay remained in the United States until his death in 1948. But his North American experience, which includes a rather prominent role in the so-called Harlem Renaissance of the 1920's, is integral to his total development as a West Indian poet. Despite a critical tradition which has tended, over the last twenty-five years, to treat his Jamaican and North American poetry as separate and exclusive entities, the fact is that McKay's literary and political involvement with the black American experience actually extends his perception of his society from a localized Jamaican focus to the dilemma of the black individual in the New World. And in turn his intensely ambivalent reactions to the United States (in his novels as well as his poetry) are related to his perception of Western culture as a whole. In short, his North American experience allowed McKay to clarify his

West Indian situation, represented by his Jamaican themes, both in its own distinctive terms and as a symbol of a New World identity and an Afro-Western continuum.

All of this underscores the inherent limitations of approaching McKay as if his poetry owes its primary or exclusive significance to a black American "protest" role. This approach is no less limiting than the popular label, "Jamaican Robert Burns," which, however unintentionally, restricts the earlier dialect poetry to some quaintly "exotic" achievement. Of course McKay himself invites the Robert Burns analogy. *Songs of Jamaica* includes a poem, "Rise and Fall," which is dedicated to Burns with apologies for making him "speak in Jamaican dialect" (*Songs of Jamaica*, p. 100). But viewed in light of his poetry as a whole McKay does not treat his art simply as an exotic Caribbean imitation of Burns' use of Scottish dialect. More pertinently, Burns is his historical precedent for developing a literary art which functions for the most part in an English literary tradition but which is rooted in idiomatic forms and cultural modes that both encompass and lie outside the English literary tradition. McKay approaches his rural dialect and its folk roots with a very conscious interest in them as structures which embody a living cultural heritage that is vitally different from his Western experience. Consequently the Jamaican's folk language and folk music have become the poet's media for the Jamaican's—and by implication, the West Indian's—hybrid identity. Later, in describing the significance of these forms in his early poetry McKay himself emphasizes the duality of his background: on the one hand, there is the pervasive folk culture of his family and rural roots, and on the other hand there is the value system imbedded in the standard English of his formal school education. Such a background both requires and facilitates rather deliberate choices. As McKay explains in his introduction to *Harlem Shadows*, his fourth collection of poetry, he always had a variety of languages from which to choose in writing his poetry. The rural dialect, various forms of folk music, and folk tales offered alternatives to the structures and materials that come with standard English.[3]

II *Dialect Verse:* Songs of Jamaica

McKay's remarks are a useful introduction to the symbolic function of language in his work, particularly the role of folk language in his dialect poetry. His language and materials are drawn directly

from a milieu upon which his poetry is imposing a shape and sense
of purpose and in which language forms reflect diverse
ethnocultural sources; a rural environment that is at once tropically
idyllic and brutally New World; and gradually stirring throughout
all of this, a nascent Jamaican identity and a faint West Indian
awareness. Viewed in this light the directions and implications of
his dialect poetry are clear enough. But the poetry is not always
successful. There is a disconcerting tendency to heighten effects
and to emphasize statements by mixing distinctive dialect forms
and folk rhythms with set poetic pieces, phrases or ab-
breviations—clichés really—from standard English. In a
hypothetical sense McKay's objectives are clear enough, even ambitious. The intermingling of forms enforces the poet's perception
of the duality that is inherent in his literary heritage (English and
Afro-Caribbean) and in his cultural milieu; and this kind of objective conforms very well with McKay's preoccupation with a sense
of aptness in choosing the diverse forms and cultural structures
which were available to him. But more often than not such intermingling merely creates a sense of jarring incongruity. Take, for
example, the absurdly obtrusive " 'twill" of "To E.M.E." in *Songs
of Jamaica*: "But when de child is gone / An' the darkness comes
on / 'Twill be anudder boy" (p. 51). In "The Hermit" the poet's
emotional tribute to the peaceful beauties of the Jamaican countryside is merely a crude patchwork of rural dialect and
Wordsworthian clichés (p. 41). And in the boisterous "My Native
Land, My Home" the energetic rhythms which celebrate a vibrant
black self-esteem collapse abruptly into the hackneyed lisping of a
highly stylized "poetic" diction (p. 51).

This marked unevenness results, in part, from the insecurity of
an inexperienced poetic imagination. At certain moments the poet
seems constrained to ensure the grand effect or the heightened
emotional appeal by falling back on the hand-me-down poetic formulae of nineteenth-century English poetry. Such uncertainty is
manifest in a poem like "De Days Dat Are Gone" where the peasant philosopher suddenly abandons his dialect style in mid-verse:
"We would be children all de time / Nor fret at childhood's pain"
(p. 59). But quite apart from the beginner's insecurity the young
McKay's uneven dialect poetry is plagued by a problem which runs
throughout this earlier body of work: he seems to lack the kind of
confidence in his idiom which is a prerequisite for truly effective
dialect verse. He clearly demonstrates a much more substantial in-

volvement in the language and experience of the folk and their dialect forms than West Indian poetry had witnessed up to that point, but the abrupt and invariably incongruous switches from dialect to standard styles suggest that he lacks confidence in his dialect forms to sustain a wide variety of intense intellectual and emotional experiences. But quite apart from these insecurities the unevenness of the dialect poetry should also be viewed in relation to McKay's calculated attempt to integrate the two rhetorical modes of his cultural heritage into a single form that would symbolize the dual nature of his background. In so doing, however, he merely undermines the realism, and with it the effectiveness of his dialect structures. The rural Jamaican folk upon whom McKay draws for his personae simply do not talk in this way. As Louise Bennett demonstrates so superbly in our own time, the speaker, in Jamaican dialect, uses or refers to the "grand" style of standard English with an underlying irony that lends itself to a barely straight-faced imitativeness or to outright laughter—while being able to function with serious fluency in standard English whenever the occasion demands it. McKay, on the other hand, is attempting to place both modes on the same level of emotional response, despite the fact that the "grand" poetic cliché is completely out of place in a context dominated by the multiple nuances (intense sorrow and joy, sarcasm, and boisterous ridicule) of the more flexible and vibrant dialect forms.

However on an even deeper level McKay's problem with the dialect style has to be explained on the basis of close involvement with his persona. In those poems which suffer from a painfully awkward mixture of styles the language may be an unrealistic way of representing the rural Jamaican peasant, but it certainly reflects the very real conflicts within McKay's own artistic personality. As a poet he is both the fiercely loyal son of the Jamaican countryside and the heir to the poetic forms of standard English. He is both the black poet-peasant and the British-educated, middleclass intellectual. This kind of personal tension, and its attendant awkwardness, are most evident in "Old England" where the poet longs to "sail athwart the ocean to hear de billows roar" and to visit the English "homeland" with its Milton, Shakespeare, Wordsworth, and Gray (pp. 63 - 65). England is the poet's homeland in the sense that it is the source of the literary heritage embodied by Milton and Shakespeare and enshrined in the pastoralism that Wordsworth bequeathed to McKay's vision of rural Jamaica. And it is equally clear that in acknowledging his English literary roots McKay feels proportionately constrained to affirm the black rural sources of his dual identity, by way of the dialect forms. In effect, that very distance from his rural roots which has been created by his middleclass education and which makes the dialect attractive to him also limits his abilities as a dialect poet. Unlike a Louise Bennett he lacks that totally empathetic personality in his art which would allow him to assume in their entirety both the folk language and the modes of perception which it embodies. In these earlier works he displays a consistent uneasiness with both of the traditions in which he attempts to work. On the whole, McKay's failures are important precisely because their underlying causes are so important in the understanding of his poetry as a whole. The early incongruity of standard poetic forms points up his unresolved relationship with that "great Western world" which is to be the focus of his characteristic ambivalence throughout his mature writing. At the same time the very unreality of dialect in "Old England" arises, as it does in "The Hermit," from the nostalgia that dominates all of his poetry; for ultimately dialect becomes a rhetorical link between the poet and the cultural sources from which he is being pushed by the very growth which shapes his total identity as poet and intellectual. And this rhetorical link is cherished and emphasized, even at the expense of his art, in direct proportion to the poet's sense of closeness to the philosophical and literary resources of the imperial "homeland."

This does not mean that McKay's standard or dialect forms are based on shallow motives. The real problem here is that he has failed to develop a satisfactory relationship between these forms in those poems in which he attempts to use them simultaneously as a way of dealing with their respective implications for his art and cultural identity. On the whole he is consistently more successful when he deals with the duality of his art and culture through one mode. In the mature poems written in the United States it is standard English that he uses, emphasizing its symbolic significance for his Western heritage and value system while subverting it from within in order to voice both his alienation from the West and his underdeveloped but nonetheless powerful sense of a coherent Afro-Western identity. In these earlier Jamaican poems he is undeniably impressive when he attempts to immerse himself in the idiom of the folk in order to describe their ambiguous situation (Western and non-Western, vibrant but impoverished, independent but brutalized) and his own duality.

"Cudjoe Fresh from de Lecture" is a fine example of this strategy. Cudjoe, a shrewd semiliterate man, is enthusiastic about the lecture on evolution and sceptical about the traditional Old Testament view: "Yes, from monkey we sprung: I believe ebery word / It long time better dan f' go say we come from mud." But if the Biblical version of the creation is unpalatable to the sceptical Cudjoe, the evolutionist logic has, historically, been fraught with distasteful implications for blacks in a white world: it seems "strange" that some lands are more "advanced" than others; Jamaicans have been fortunate in having been taken to "a blessed place as dis a ya," for instead of living as half-naked Africans driving cattle for white men they were now civilized (pp. 57 - 58). Cudjoe's rural folk background provides McKay with an effectively satiric distance from the theology and symbolism of white Christianity. At the same time the speaker's semiliterate enthusiasm for the evolutionist's viewpoint results in an unconsciously subversive naiveté: the popular image of evolution ("from monkey we sprung") echoes a popular Western image of Africans as monkeys. In this context the evolutionist's universal "we" assumes a wryly ethnic significance. Altogether, Cudjoe's forthright blend of scepticism and naiveté allows McKay to affirm simultaneously a strong attachment to the rationalism of Western science (versus the dogma of Biblical faith) and to underscore the essential irrationality of Western racism. In the same vein Cudjoe's fierce allegiance to Jamaica is an extension of McKay's nationalism and of the poet's irrevocably Western sensibilities; but at the same time Cudjoe's slurs on Africa demonstrate the price of self-hate which the unaware black pays for that kind of Western sensibility. And even more incisively, this self-hate involves a pathetic ignorance, or self-deception about the West Indian's own condition: Cudjoe's image of "uncibilized" half-naked Africans passes over the fact that in his own "blessed" Jamaica blacks do drive the white man's cattle. Nor does this exhaust the multiple connotations of the persona's language. On the one hand, Jamaica is "blessed," to return to Cudjoe's phrase, by nature and by the vitality of the rural folk whom Cudjoe himself represents. But on the other hand those blessings are tempered by the racial realities of the Jamaican's Western world and by the fact that a certain kind of ignorance or naiveté is the price that we sometimes pay for our notions of idyllic innocence. Indeed McKay invokes the idyllic image of the pastoral in order to demonstrate its limitations. Clearly this is a far cry from the old Caribbean pastoral. The poet can now celebrate the beauties of his landscape without necessarily lapsing into the banal escapism of that pastoral tradition. Consequently he is aware of the pluses and minuses of those idealized black roots, in much the same way that he is sensitive to the ambiguities of his relationship with that Western heritage.

Altogether "Cudjoe" demonstrates the complex, even paradoxical insights which McKay effects through his dialect form at its best. And in this regard the poem reflects the diversity of his best work in *Songs of Jamaica*. There is the uninhibited celebration of rural life in "Me Bannabees" where the abundance of the bonavist pea (bannabees) harvest symbolizes the individual vitality and social well-being of McKay's peasant persona. "King Banana" continues the harvest motif in a similar vein, pitting the black ("naygur") small farmer's self-sufficiency and ethnic pride against the strange world of the white ("buccra") agronomist. But this celebration of the peasant life is countered in "Out of Debt" by a numbing sense of poverty which transforms the mere experience of being out of debt into a Yuletide triumph of sorts. And lest the reader entertain a nice romantic antithesis between rural paradise and urban degeneracy, both "Little Jim" and "Jim at Sixteen" use the countryside and the city as settings for physical hardship, crime, and guilt. Similarly, the city prostitute's rage at injustice ("A Midnight Woman to the Bobby") invites comparison with the black small farmer's understated bitterness at the white landowner's entrenched privilege ("Quashie to Buccra"). There is the pointed contrast between a relatively unspoilt countryside and the degenerate city, especially when poems like "Me Bannabees" and "Jim at Sixteen" are read together. But on the whole these clearcut contrasts exist side by side with that pervasive sense of a universal malaise which becomes so pronounced in the later poetry, and which appears in this first collection in a work like "Wha' fe Do?" For in this poem all the ills of racism, poverty, social injustice, and ill-luck are all part of a hostile and inescapable order of things which must be viewed with a sense of resignation.

On the whole the relative diversity of experiences and judgments which these poems represent attests to the flexibility and responsiveness which McKay does discover in his dialect forms in his more effective use of the folk idiom. At such times he avoids the limited, and limiting, tactic of assigning exclusive kinds of insights to dialect and standard English respectively, a tactic which clearly backfires in "Old England," for example. Another key to his successes in *Songs of Jamaica* lies in his ear for folk music and dance, as well as for the dialect itself. In "Me Bannabees" the joyous shay-shay rhythms of the "yard" song imitate the frenzied growth and sheer abundance of the bonavist pea. Those rhythms are also appropriate because the poem's celebration of the plenty of farm life is also the celebration of life itself: the dance rhythms and the seasonal cycle of growth merge into one as the symbol of the life principle. And this emphasis on the life principle is reinforced by the characteristic hyperboles of the dialect, especially in so far as they evoke a sense of abundance: "De blossom draw the bees / Same how de soup draw man / Some call it 'broke-pot' peas" (p. 15). In "King Banana" the harvest-as-life celebration is tempered by the sobering realities that are invoked by the collo-quial style. The peasant's favorite self-description, "naygur," is a defiantly ironic adoption of the old racial slur as an emblem of ethnic pride; and as such it is coupled with its colloquial counter-part, "buccra," which now becomes a mockingly subversive reference to the all-knowing, all-powerful white overlord. The colloquial structure therefore counterbalances the poet's temptation to celebrate a pastoral idyll: the pointed reminders of racial and class distinctions counteract the opening images of an abundant and unspoiled paradise; but these reminders also heighten the speaker's need to celebrate his individualistic vitality and to transcend his limiting environment. Finally, the note of protest which is implied by McKay's colloquial structure becomes more overt in the per-sona's direct attack on those who contribute to their economic dis-advantages in an unequal society by spending their share of the banana harvest-sales in drink.

The protest in "King Banana" is effective even when it is ob-trusive because it enriches the poem's emotive texture by varying the reader's responses (joyousness and regret) to the work as a whole. On the other hand the emotional appeal of "Little Jim" is effectively limited. The poem is really a sustained scream of agony. Little Jim's ulcerated leg symbolizes the decidedly unidyllic side of the rural life. But even here the emotional appeal of the poem is less limited than it seems on the surface; for McKay's effective use of the dialect-as-scream depends on the implicit evocation of those happy and innocent images that are implied by the rural reference and by the title's suggestion of a youthful vulnerability, a fragile innocence. The fragility of our pastoral fantasies is clear enough to McKay whose pastoral dialect poems are essentially antipastoral.

This fragility is heightened by the mournful chant of "Hard
Times," a work in which McKay draws on the slow rhythms of the
rural "wake" songs to suggest the numbing monotony and
repetitiveness of poverty—notwithstanding the incongruousness of
his rhyme scheme. In rejecting the insubstantial visions of the older
pastoral tradition McKay emphasizes the real strengths of his
Jamaican peasant. Even the bleak vision of a universal malaise in
"Wha' fe Do?" eventually gives way to the resilience of McKay's
peasant persona, and that resilience is suggested by a bouyant
country-dance rhythm which still manages to be effective despite
the stultifying rhyme scheme of McKay's dialect verse. In this
regard the bouyant resiliency of "Wha' fe Do?" draws upon a
rhetorical tradition which has been strongly entrenched in the
language and art forms of the folk: the statement of hardship and
suffering is couched in an ebullient style which not only voices a
defiant sense of life and dignity, but also mocks the outsider's guilty need to believe that the poor actually enjoy their poverty. In
"Fetchin' Water," for example, McKay's persona comments on the
insensitive pleasure that the white tourist derives from watching
the poor at their everyday chores, and offers a telling contrast
between the cool comforts of the outsider and the hot, tiring
drudgery of fetching water. The contrast is underlined by one of
those numerous proverbs which are typical of the rural folk idiom
and upon which McKay draws freely. The white tourist enjoys the
cool comforts of a stone on the sea bed, in contrast with the rock
which must suffer the blaze of the sun: " 'Nuff rock'tone in de sea,
yet none / But those 'pon lan' know 'bouten sun" (p. 42).

This is the kind of contrast that is underlined by the precise antitheses which McKay discovers in yet another set of folk proverbs
and which Quashie uses to the same purpose in "Quashie to Buccra":

> You tas'e petater an' you say it sweet
> But you no know how hard we wuk fe it. . . .
> De sun hot like when fire ketch a town;
> Shade-tree look temptin', yet we caan' lie down. . . .
> You see petater tear up groun', you run. (pp. 13 - 14)

The flamboyant hyperbole emphasizes the plenty of a good
harvest. But on an ironic level it is part of the rhetorical mask
which McKay finds ready-made for his social satire in his dialect

forms. For while the hyperbole as a whole celebrates plenty and gives voice to the speaker's vitality, the specific phrase, "tear up," implies both the welcome crush of abundance and the impact of the social inequities which allow buccra the exclusive prerogatives of a comfortable shade-tree existence. The sweet potato itself becomes a symbolic extension of Quashie's satirical style. The sweetness or vitality of Quashie's spirit is both a reflection of his actual bouyancy in the face of adversity and the smiling mask which he offers to ridicule and satisfy buccra's guilty expectations. This mask, the mask of language, excites buccra's laughter because he is unprepared to accept the bitter hardness of the sweet potato as a fact. And Quashie's rhetoric exploits the advantages of this mask as a covert protest against privilege and injustice.

The dialect forms with which McKay works in this first collection of poetry do not only offer the understated ironies of the rhetorical mask. They are also rich in the straightforward expletive, in the uninhibited abuse which McKay also adapts for his satiric viewpoint. The prostitute's tongue-lashing of the policeman in "A Midnight Woman to the Bobby" is a case in point. Her harsh vituperative style, complete with spectacular insults, is the poet's medium for a direct attack on the abuses of power (by the police and law courts in this instance) and on the poverty which drives women like the persona to prostitution: "No palm me up, you dutty brute, / You' jam mout' mash like ripe bread-fruit" (p. 74). But at the same time the unrelieved harshness of the language reflects the speaker's own brutishness. If the policeman is a bullying brute who represents the official abuses of power, the speaker herself is a brute, the end product of her brutalizing environment. And although the typical incongruities of the dialect imagery create their usual comic effects, they also reflect adversely on the speaker. In this case the startling juxtaposition which compares the policeman with an overripe breadfruit—with *objects*—also confirms the prostitute's own fall from humanity to objecthood. This double exposure of both the system and its victims links the early satire of "Midnight Woman" with the later protest poetry in that the poet's double-edged irony underscores the blunted humanity of both the established order and its victims. And together with the more subtle ironies of "Quashie to Buccra" and the music rhythms of poems like "Me Bannabees," works such as "Midnight Woman" demonstrate the extent to which McKay's early poetic styles evolve from the discovery and adaptation of structures and rhetorical traditions within the dialect. In demonstrating and exploiting the variety of structural choices within the dialect he is clearly superior as a dialect poet to any of his contemporaries, notwithstanding the equally obvious limitations of his dialect art.

The satiric modes of *Songs of Jamaica* look forward to the use of dialect as the language of satire in the next collection, *Constab Ballads*. But there is one poem which is unique in *Songs of Jamaica* in that it is the only one of the collection written wholly in standard English and which has important implications for McKay's later development as a poet. "Strokes of the Tamarind Switch" is perhaps the most direct and outraged statement of protest in the collection. Written after McKay joined the police force, it voices his concern at the barbarities, especially whipping, which were often sanctioned in the name of justice and which eventually contributed to his decision to leave the force. The poem's language evokes the violence of its subject, the graphic effectiveness that marks the poems on racial conflict in his North American years:

> The cutting tamarind switch
> Had left its bloody mark
> And on his legs were streaks
> That looked like boiling bark. (p. 111)

The violence of the punishment evokes the brutishness of the social inequities which "goaded" the young criminal "to wrong;" and it is matched by the intense pain of the poet's own compassion ("my bosom burned"). McKay's choice of standard English for this poem heightens its special, even isolated, significance as a protest poem in the collection as a whole. But more importantly, the choice of standard English is itself as thematically significant as the dialect structures and folk forms of the other poems. Like his mature protest works in later years, the use of standard English here is fundamental to the ironic design of his art: the brutality of the established order and its essentially noncivilized values are exposed through the very medium—its language—which it holds up to the illiterate (non-white) world as the norm of civilized excellence. In a more personal sense standard English is also integral to the young McKay's poetic self-consciousness, to his awareness of the cultural tensions between his black peasant roots and the white Western world. His self-conflict is centered on his role in a middleclass milieu, as poet and police officer, and on his empathy with the victims of the Western-oriented, middleclass establishment.

The selection of standard English therefore goes hand in hand with a highly personal tone that identifies the poet very closely with the voice of the poem:

> I dared not look at him,
> My eyes with tears were dim
> My spirit filled with hate
> Of man's depravity,
> I hurried through the gate. (p. 111)

The language and style emphasize the poet's identification with the established order, not only by virtue of his official role, but also on the basis of his mastery of buccra's language and literature. And in this latter connection, even the highly conventional poetic diction simultaneously reinforces the image of his intimacy with established convention and implies an awkwardness, a sense of unease. His physical withdrawal from the flogging symbolizes a sense of alienation from the criminal, not only as criminal, but also as one who shares his racial and cultural roots. The consistent use of standard English to the end confirms this felt distance between McKay and the victim. But the reader is left with the impression of a deep-seated tension rather than a complete withdrawal. The satiric intensity of the language represents a corresponding detachment from the established order even as he continues to function within it and with its language. Conversely, the poet-constable does return, eventually, to console the prisoner at the end of the flogging. And finally, the poem as a whole does represent the poet's determination to return to the prisoner's world in a larger sense—a return to commitment and awareness.

On the whole, the standard English of this poem allows McKay to elaborate on those ambiguities and tensions which are also evident in the relationship between a white Western value system and the black rural poor in the dialect poems. But he does so with an intensely personal directness that never really appears in the dialect poems, and it is on this basis that "Tamarind Switch" is so significant in McKay's development. As has already been suggested, he fails to be effective whenever he attempts to explore the poet's personality by way of an incongruous and wholly unconvincing amalgamation of standard poetic forms and folk idiom. He is far more convincing in "Tamarind Switch" because he is functioning within a language with which, for better or worse, he is clearly more comfortable. His tools have immersed him, as poet and intellectual, in Western literary traditions, Western language forms, and a Western-oriented middleclass value system; and in the process they have created a distance between him and the other tools which are embodied in the peasant culture of his rural past. Even at his most effective moments as a dialect poet McKay never really bridges that gap. On the other hand, as a dissident poet and intellectual he is engaged in a ceaseless conflict with the Western sources of his intellectuality; and he is most effective when he places that conflict in the very arena—standard English—that symbolizes both his intimacy with and reserve about his Western heritage as a whole. In this arena he is the archetypal West Indian Caliban seizing Prospero's language in his rebellion, albeit an undeveloped one, against Prospero. On this basis "Tamarind Switch" links *Songs of Jamaica* directly with *Harlem Shadows* and other later poems.

III   *Dialect Verse:* Constab Ballads

The effectiveness of "Tamarind Switch," written wholly in standard English, should not minimize the significance of McKay's development in his second dialect collection *Constab Ballads*. This collection continues McKay's exploration of social injustice and racial inequities through the distinctive forms of his folk idiom. Here his treatment of the disadvantaged as both victims and brutes extends the thematic emphases of *Songs of Jamaica* while anticipating the directions of his social and racial satire in his American poetry. And the pejorative images of the white buccra in *Songs of Jamaica* merge into the more fully developed, wideranging attack on the social order as a whole which is to dominate the satire of the more mature poems. Both his development as a poet and his short-lived career as a police officer have hardened McKay's scepticism about the social structure as such, and that scepticism finds a voice in the author's preface to *Constab Ballads* as he reflects wryly on his decision to leave the constabulary: he was disqualified by his "most improper sympathy with wrongdoers" and by "a fierce hatred of injustice" (pp. 7 - 8). Moreover, as a policeman in the city McKay experiences his second, more direct level of involvement with racial conflict. The poet-policeman who must often bear the brunt of black suspicion because of the very fact that he is a policeman working for the white power structure is more directly confronted with the harsh demands of racial conflict and racial allegiance than are any of the figures in *Songs of Jamaica*. Consequently, there is less use of the subtle ironies of the smiling mask, and a correspondingly greater reliance on the straightforward outcry which appeared earlier in poems like "Midnight Woman" and which is to dominate the *Harlem Shadows* volume. On the whole the choice of the policeman persona is more than an autobiographical coincidence. The character's black, rural, peasant background offers a strong bond with the poor and the criminal, even when they reject him as a representative of the establishment. And conversely, it places him, on a personal level, in conflicts—with whites and superiors—which are really external versions of the self-conflicts that are intrinsic to his middleclass status.

The intensification of satiric protest in this volume goes hand in hand with a corresponding emphasis on the romantic idealization of the countryside. The hills of rural Jamaica and the life of the farmer are the recurrent subjects of a nostalgia that obviously compensates for the poet's revulsion at the city, especially in the lovesick longings of "Last Words of the Dying Recruit," "The Heart of a Constab," and "The Labourer's Life Give Me." This does not mean that McKay's second collection has lapsed into the simplistic antithesis of countryside-versus-city which the first collection successfully avoids. After all, *Constab Ballads* offers one of McKay's most disturbing images of peasant brutality in "Cotch Donkey," in which the peasant wreaks upon his donkey his frustrations and anger as the perennial whipping-post and beast-of-burden in his society. And the joyous celebration of countryside living are clearly parallelled in the volume by the *joie de vivre* of a police band marching through the city ("Route March") and by the carnival gaiety of Saturday night in the city ("Papine Corner"). But on the whole the essential ambiguity of the countryside in *Songs of Jamaica* is giving way, with time and distance, to the decidedly more sentimental perspectives of urban exile, in much the same way that Jamaica as a whole assumes an unspoilt pastoral image from the distance of North America in *Harlem Shadows*.

IV   Harlem Shadows: *McKay's North American Experience*

That pastoral image results from the nostalgic treatment of his Jamaican past in *Harlem Shadows*. On the whole the nostalgic poetry is uneven. McKay frequently lapses into a self-indulgent sentimentality in works like "Summer Moon in New Hampshire" and "Home Thoughts." And in the highly popular but insubstantial "Spanish Needle" this sentimentality is linked with the kind of Wordsworthian excesses that characterized so many of McKay's nineteenth-century predecessors. However, at the same time the nostalgic images of Jamaica are also central to McKay's rather complex awareness about the ambiguities and self-conflicts of the West Indian artist in exile from his Caribbean roots, and the black Westerner's sense of both belonging and alienation. And on this level the nostalgia for rural Jamaica and the pastoral mode is used by McKay with the same degree of sophisticated self-consciousness that marks his exploitation of the pastoral tradition in the earlier dialect poetry. The popular "Flame-heart" is a good example of this self-consciousness. The poem opens with very strong echoes of Wordsworth's "Tintern Abbey": "So much have I forgotten in ten years / So much in ten brief years!" But these echoes are followed immediately by the decidedly Jamaican image of the "shy forget-me-not." The juxtaposition of the Jamaican image and the Western (Wordsworthian) reference points up McKay's double irony. The exile's forgetfulness of his Jamaican roots contradicts the perennial resolution to remember. In cultural terms his forgetfulness is part of the Western heritage that is represented by his poetic mode, complete with its echoes of Wordsworth; but at the same time this mode (like the earlier dialect mode) must be exploited to affirm roots which must not be forgotten if the poet is to preserve a sense of moral and ethnic wholeness that embraces his Afro-Caribbean as well as Western sources. Conversely, an exclusive immersion in a nostalgia for the rural Jamaican roots is a species of escape from what the poet has inevitably become—he is now the complex figure of the Jamaican in exile in North America and, more crucially, the black artist in the West. Hence the pastoral innocence (or seeming innocence) upon which his nostalgia for Jamaica focuses is palpably fragile, even limited, despite its poignant beauty: "We were so happy, happy, I remember, / Beneath the poinsettia's red in warm December" (pp. 9 - 10). Innocent happiness of this kind is limited because it is really a youthful inexperience.

Yet exile is not merely a mode of forgetfulness but, in a more important, psychological sense, it is also a catalyst which crystallizes the West Indian's identity in the West, the kind of catalyst which McKay explores through the pastoral themes of "The Easter Flower," "My Mother," and "Adolescence." In "North and South" the negative as well as positive implications of exile are frankly derived from a highly suggestive context of dreams: "O sweet are tropic lands for waking dreams! / There time and life move lazily along" (p. 17). In one sense this longing is an affirmation of the poet's allegiance to his Jamaican identity, a symbolic return to his Afro-Caribbean roots. But in another, more suspect, sense the image of lazy, unspoilt tropic lands exactly reproduces those white tourist assumptions which are attacked in earlier poems like "Fetchin' Water." And on this basis the image reinforces the suspicion that "dreams" are, simultaneously, the exile's natural longing and the fantasies of the white outsider. Moreover, the association of the exile's images with the outsider's perspectives reinforces that sense of distance, or uprootedness, which initially inspires the nostalgic need to reaffirm one's cultural roots.

In these poems the experience of nostalgia is rather more complex than the sentimental regrets and longings of *Constab Ballads*. Here nostalgia opens the door for the poet's frank, even relentless, self-exploration as artist and black Jamaican. And that self-exploration assumes West Indian, rather than specifically Jamaican, dimensions in those nostalgic poems in which McKay modifies an exclusive emphasis on the idealistic recall of the past in favor of a precise but ironic antithesis between North America and the West Indies. "Subway Wind" is one such poem, portraying the American city as a sepulcher, which contrasts with the poet's memories of the Caribbean's "lofty palm trees blooming white" (p. 54). Similar contrasts are offered by "Winter in the Country" and "When Dawn Comes to the City." In these works the experience of exile from the Caribbean expands McKay's sense of Afro-Caribbean roots from a strictly Jamaican to an inclusive West Indian context. In recoiling from the city and its sepulchral subway he reaches back, not to Jamaica as such, but to "the islands," to the West Indies. His persona is now the archetypal West Indian who has dominated the imagination of West Indian writers, especially since the Second World War: exile from the Caribbean stimulates the discovery and articulation of a distinctive West Indian consciousness. The ironic dimensions of the exile's contrast between North America and the islands are equally significant for the exile's ethnic consciousness. On the one hand, the decided preference for the West Indian experience is fraught with those ambiguities attributable to McKay's nostalgia for cultural roots. And on the other hand, the fierce contempt for the United States and all its works is tempered by a delightfully perverse satisfaction with the catalyst that his American milieu offers for his continuing self-realization.

Indeed that contempt is even tempered, in poems like "To One Coming North," by a grudging admiration for the distinctive, though frequently elusive, beauties of the "North."

This introduces a central paradox in McKay's poetry on the United States. White racism and the general harshness of the city are both oppressive and stimulating. The very ugliness of the city challenges the really resilient spirit to discover and celebrate beauty in these unpromising surroundings. In other words, it demands from the poet himself the very kind of resilience and bouyancy which attract him, in his dialect poetry, to the personality of his Jamaican folk. Moreover, all those forces which are symbolized by the city—indifference, racial animosity, technological coldness—inspire a rebelliousness that affirms the poet's "dark"—racial, hidden—needs. In the words of "Dawn in New York," when dawn comes to the city "I go darkly-rebel to my work" (p. 43). In "America" his adopted country is the beloved hell that tests his self-awareness, and in "White City" white racism is the catalyst for an intense ethnic consciousness. Indeed there is a puritanic streak of sorts in McKay at this stage of his development which anticipates his eventual religious fervor and which, at this point, allows him to welcome racial suffering as a kind of crucible. The victim of white racism assumes the identity of a martyr. In "The Lynching," for example, he is even Christ-like. And in the famous "Baptism" the paradox of triumph-in-suffering is inherent in the familiar motif of trial by fire: "I will come out, back to your world of tears, / A stronger soul within a finer frame" (p. 52)

In these poems dealing with McKay's relationship with North America language itself becomes as much of a major cultural symbol as it is in his earlier, Jamaican poetry. Here his ambivalence towards America and its white urban culture is voiced in a language which demonstrates once again the complex nature of his relationship with his English language and his English literary forms. Consequently that paradox noted in his overall treatment of the American presence is matched by another, the paradox of satirically exploiting his Western forms as anti-Western modes. The black Christ figure of "The Lynching" is an archetypal extension of this process. Like the black Christ of much black American literature McKay's archetype taunts the Christian West for having betrayed the Christian ideal, for it in effect seeks to demonstrate the Christ-like innocence and moral superiority of the West's black victim. Similarly the very fabric of his poetic diction serves the dual purpose of confirming the poet's share in the Western literary heritage and voicing his rejection of the West's antihumanist traditions. The choice of the sonnet form for works like "America" or "If We must Die" is significant in this regard. The sonnet form, laden with centuries-old connotations of love and human idealism in Western literature is now the medium that describes the hatreds of racism and exploitation. Moreover, McKay carefully manipulates his language in order to create the kind of verbal texture that is fundamental to his satiric subversiveness. "America," for example, unfolds through a series of images which confirm the size and power of the awesome American presence ("tiger's tooth," "vigor," "bigness," "might and granite") but which lead inexorably to the vision of America's inevitable moral malaise—"Like priceless treasures sinking in the sand." At the same time the poem's contrapuntal structure presents America's black victim as a figure of growth that contrasts with America's decline (p. 6).

"The White City" reveals the black poet as the archetypal Caliban manipulating his Western language, and in the process effecting a pointed reversal of racial terminology. Thus "dark Passion" is no longer a negative term rooted in the notion of blackness as a Satanic symbol. The poem offers the very concept of dark passions as the positive assertion of the black poet's ethnic and hitherto secret (that is, "dark") humanity; and in so doing it opposes the whiteness which is no longer the invariable symbol of virtue but which has become a symbol of hell, "the white world's hell," in a racial sense (p. 23). "The White House," published after the *Harlem Shadows* collection, exemplifies the precisely balanced phrasing that reflects the clear-cut ethnic divisions in the poem. The "shut door" of the white house is matched by the "tightened face" of the black persona's reaction. The glass of the "boldly" shining door suggests the fragile nature of the bold facade of white self-importance, and in turn that fragility is neatly counterbalanced by the imagined violence of the black as "chafing savage" and by the very real power of black anger. Moreover, the images of the "chafing savage" walking on the "decent street" of the white neighborhood pinpoint the simplistic antitheses which the occupant of the white house applies to the complex tensions between black and white. But in the poem's finale the mocking images of white decency and black savagery are explicitly reversed. In keeping with the McKay ethic of strength-through-suffering, it is the black figure who now represents real restraint rather than a glass-brittle strength. And in the process the notion of the law as white restraint is exposed as a mere pretense:

> I must search for wisdom every hour,
> Deep in my wrathful bosom sore and raw,
> And find in it the superhuman power
> To hold me to the letter of your law! (*Selected Poems*, p. 78).

To be held to the "letter" of the law is to make the word of Western morality and law an effective truth rather than a "shining" but fragile decency. It is also part of the broad and fundamental process by which the poet's satire subverts the conventional *practices* of Western culture by seizing upon and reaffirming the neglected ideals of Western humanism. And finally, it is an extension of the manner in which McKay uses the inherited "letter" of Western literature to reaffirm his complex relationship with the West.

This is the kind of reaffirmation that motivates the use of language and symbols in "The Lynching." The archetype of the black Christ has a calculated shock effect in that it implies a rejection of the white Christian's conventionally white image of the Christ figure. The lynching therefore becomes a crucifixion and it invests the perverted Christianity of the West with a barbaric, even Satanic, image. Moreover the reversal of images is supplemented by the juxtaposition of distinct time references. The Nativity star now hovers over the crucifixion scene: "All night a bright and solitary star . . . / Hung pitifully o'er the swinging char." In turn the sense of dislocation which results from this juxtaposition is reinforced by the telling combination of the highly stylized diction ("o'er") and the grisly novelty of "char." Moreover, the Nativity symbolism now has two, ironically balanced, implications: it heralds the birth of black strength through suffering and it is also a grisly, sarcastic salute to the next generation of anti-Christs—the "little lads, lynchers that were to be," dancing around the corpse. Finally, this inversion of the Nativity symbol and of the traditional image of childhood innocence is linked with the reversal of conventional day-night, life-death symbols. Thus the dawn brings with it the confirmation of the victim's physical death and his persecutors' moral self-destruction; "Day dawned and soon the mixed crowds came to view / The ghastly body swinging in the sun" (*Harlem Shadows*, p. 51).

V   *McKay's Ambiguity: Commitment and Isolation*

This kind of satiric inversion is even more direct in the poems published after the *Harlem Shadows* collection in response to McKay's growing commitment to Roman Catholicism. Hence in "Look Within," written during the Second World War, the devout Christian joins the poet in damning Western hypocrisy—with the rhetoric of Western Christianity. But it is in the *Harlem Shadows* poems that the ironic manipulation of language and symbolism most effectively demonstrates that sense of ambiguity discussed in the earlier poetry and which links McKay with modern West Indian poetry. The *Harlem Shadows* poem, "Outcast," is McKay's most effective analysis of that duality. On the one hand, the "great western world" holds him "in fee" permanently, but on the other hand, his spirit longs for an African past which, admittedly, he cannot even visualize in emotionally immediate terms. There is no sentimental nostalgia here. The poet has no illusions about being intimate with the African past. Thus the poem's structure is based on a sustained tension between a hard-headed realism about the poet's place in the West and a firm grasp of the strengths as well as limits of his non-Western allegiances. And the ambiguities of his position are reflected in the multiple meanings of the poem's language. Africa is now "dim," or forgotten as a result of his historical place in the West where Africa can only be seen as "dim," or savagely mysterious. The double connotations of Africa's "dim" image represent the poet's conflicting reaction to Africa—an Afro-Caribbean yearning countered by a Western ignorance or indifference. Similarly, his complaint that his spirit is "bondaged" by his body in his spiritual quest for an African identity holds a double emphasis. The more obvious reference to the physical and cultural barriers between himself and Africa is supplemented by the implication that he himself has participated in a kind of intellectual bondage which is really an extension of physical slavery. The interweaving of his Western sensibilities and his non-Western yearnings reaches its climax in the pivotal eighth line of the sonnet: he portrays himself on bended knees to the "alien gods" of the West. The phrasing accepts the irrevocable nature of the Western texture of his identity. But that acceptance strains against the self-revulsion which interprets his Western personality as a sign of slavish loyalty, even as a kind of heresy: the Westerner's familiar description of non-Christian cultures as pagan societies symbolized by "alien gods" has now been turned against the West itself. The semantic gesture both enforces the poet's anti-Western spirit and confirms his intimacy with Western modes of perception and self-expression. He is as much the son of the West as he is its rebel.

He therefore remains effectively an outcast from both the West and Africa. He is a wandering "ghost," a "thing apart" who was born "Under the white man's menace, out of time." The phrase, "out of time," concludes the poem with a cluster of meanings which intensify the theme of isolation. He has been born out of time, not in the Western sense of an African without history, but in the sense that the history of blacks in the West has deprived him of a dynamic continuity with an African past. In musical terms the Afro-Western history of dislocation, slavery, and racial injustice represents a disharmony, a disruptiveness, which is analogous to being out of musical time and which has inspired the poet's wistful longing for a cultural heritage that he has lost ("My soul would sing forgotten jungle songs"). To be "out of time" is to be out of step, to be isolated from those others who enjoy a tangible sense of cultural continuity.

But, in turn, this complex of negative responses to the experience of isolation is finally counterbalanced by a more positive and creative self-perception which is inherent in the poem, or more precisely, in the dynamic functions of the poetic imagination itself. In this sense, being isolated is not a mere negative but really a condition of one's perceptive detachment from one's environment, the kind of detachment which allows the poet to comprehend his experience in all its complexity and contradictions. Hence, in the final analysis "Outcast" is not simply an exploration of the perennially divided archetype of the outcast. It is also a demonstration of that creative energy which allows the archetype, but more specifically the artist-as-outcast, to transcend the disruptive consequences of an outcast history. In effect, the duality of the poem itself—a Western form, the sonnet, adopted for a specifically Afro-Western vision—is an artistic form; and as such it is an harmonious structure which represents the poet's role in transforming the fragmentation of the outcast past into a dynamic and essentially integrated kind of dualism (*Harlem Shadows*, p. 45).

This kind of dualism also accounts for the consistent theme of isolation which runs through McKay's treatment of other blacks. For on this interpersonal level McKay displays both a yearning to be with and a sense of separation from the unlettered and generally disadvantaged blacks of his poems. The poet himself and his readers cannot escape the gulf which seems to widen between McKay's subjects and his middleclass status and intellectual experience. At its best and its worst the dialect poetry represents a formal, aesthetic attempt to bridge the gap. And if the troublesome unevenness of his dialect attests to his general failure to bridge the gap convincingly, the precise brilliance of "Outcast" represents a mature ability to confront and deal honestly with that gulf. For in the long run no one is more aware than McKay himself of his divided response to his black roots and to his fellow blacks. He is fully aware but isolated, a self-conscious "thing apart" not only from the West and from the African past, but also from his fellow Jamaicans as a police officer in *Constab Ballads*, from the American city as a Jamaican in "On Broadway," and from the black American as a black poet and intellectual in "Harlem Shadows" and "The Harlem Dancer." In a very important sense McKay's development as a poet can be perceived as a continuing process of resolving his lifelong sense of isolation. He attempts to do this through the moral sympathies and the folk idiom of the dialect poetry. And in *Harlem Shadows* the fierce intensity of his protest art maintains his moral and ethnic sympathies at the same time that he develops his art, in "Outcast," for example, into a process which enables him to experience isolation as the positive, even creative, function of his dual identity.

But notwithstanding the artistic triumph of "Outcast" and the moral and ethnic certitudes of the poem's total effect, McKay never really accepts the kind of dualism that is inherent even in a redefined outcast role. He continues to be nagged by the suspicion that his isolation represents an incompleteness rather than an identifiable and creative distinctiveness. And in the poems written after the publication of *Harlem Shadows* that suspicion seems to have grown into a conviction. Religious faith is now the alternative to the delicate balance and complex self-consciousness of the black outcast role. "The Negro's Tragedy" defines the limits of white perception: "There is no white man who could write my book." But the alternative commitment is not to blacks but to God: "This Negro laughs and prays to God for Light" (*Selected Poems*, p. 50). This double withdrawal from both black and white, and in the process from the entire ethnocultural issue, is very explicit in "The Pagan Isms": "And so to God I go to make my peace, / Where black nor white can follow to betray" (*Selected Poems*, p. 49). Such a deliberate withdrawal has to be distinguished from the duality which evolves from *Songs of Jamaica* through to *Harlem Shadows*, and with it McKay abandons that quest for an ethnocultural wholeness which forms much of his artistic development. But on balance that quest remains unquestionably as the single most important impulse in his poetry, for it allows him to represent the Jamaican poet as a microcosm of the West Indian experience as a whole: a rural folk culture with distinct, albeit half-understood, echoes of an African continuity; the countervailing weight of a Western heritage; and finally, the groping for a distinctive identity which harmonizes the diverse, often conflicting sources into an identifiable wholeness. Given its scope and directions, this quest actually represents a tentative but important shift towards a poetic and ethnic consciousness that is now assuming a West Indian character while celebrating its specific territorial origins. On all counts the quest represents the most ambitious and innovative undertaking by a West Indian poet up to that point, bearing in mind that this had all been accomplished by the time of the publication of *Harlem Shadows* in 1922. Despite all the unevenness that accomplishment remains McKay's most important contribution to West Indian poetry.

CHAPTER 3

The Emergence of Modern West Indian Poetry: 1940 - 1960

1. Major Themes

THE three decades after the outbreak of the Second World War were a period of remarkable activity in West Indian poetry, remarkable in that the fairly large number of vigorous and innovative writers offers such a striking contrast with the prevailing mediocrity of the earlier periods. This is the period in which West Indian poetry began to attract serious critical attention, in a far cry from the condescending chuckles with which the intelligentsia of eighteenth-century London greeted the absurdities of Grainger's Caribbean "Georgics." The founding of literary magazines like *Bim* and *Kyk-over-al* by Frank Collymore and A. J. Seymour, respectively, symptomizes the strong local committment to the *idea* of an emerging body of literature—West Indian literature. And in turn this idea is encouraged by the magazines' support of both new and established writers. Consequently writers like Jamaica's George Campbell, in the 1940's, and Guyana's Martin Carter, in the 1950's, each represents his generation's new urgency, a vigorous awareness of his local Caribbean situation, and the insistence on the West Indian experience as one that is both distinctive and symptomatic of the human condition as a whole. In turn, the 1960's are the period that witnesses the emergence of major writers like Derek Walcott and Edward Brathwaite whose work, together with that of their contemporaries, has already guaranteed that the prolific energies of the last thirty-five years will remain unabated in the foreseeable future. In fact many of those energies are still very active in that several of the more important postwar writers are still active in the postcolonial period. Andrew Salkey who is better known as a novelist and essayist published his long, continuous

63

work *Jamaica* in 1973. A. J. Seymour continues to produce a succession of poetry pamphlets after thirty-eight years of publishing. Similarly A. L. Hendriks' *These Green Islands* (1971) and Anthony LaRose's *Foundations* (1966) are really the continuation of individual activity that goes back to the 1940's and 1950's.

If there is a danger in emphasizing the productivity and imaginative freshness of the postwar period it lies in the temptation to perceive these new energies as an unexpected phenomenon and the poets themselves as the unheralded pioneers of a new West Indian literary tradition. But in the first place these energies are not limited to the poets but are also manifest in the outpouring of creative and critical writing by the essayists, dramatists, and novelists who were supported by *Bim, Kyk-over-al, Focus* and other local publications. Secondly, although the nineteenth and early twentieth centuries are a veritable wasteland in contrast with the postwar period it is both possible and historically important to recognize a continuity, particularly between the few significant writers of the preceding generations and their successors. The postwar protests against social and racial injustice have their antecedents in the work of Claude McKay and Una Marson. As I have already suggested Walter M. Lawrence's poetry establishes a pattern for modern West Indian poetry in its grasp of a West Indian experience that demonstrated both its distinctive nuances and its symbolic significance for a genuine—rather than narrowly Eurocentric—notion of universality. In noting the intense anticolonial temper of the postwar generation it is also necessary to recall the uneven but significant anticolonial themes of Lawrence or Egbert Martin. And the more innovative work of Claude McKay and Una Marson anticipates the younger generation's conscious attempts to break the psychological and literary stranglehold of the colonial Caribbean pastoral by developing innovative forms in both standard English and folk idioms.

There is a corresponding continuity in the sociopolitical experiences of the earlier generations and the new breed. The nineteenth-century decline of the sugar plantation economy, particularly after the abolition of slavery, was exacerbated by Great Britain's growing indifference to the welfare of its increasingly unprofitable West Indian holdings. Consequently Egbert Martin's impassioned poems on behalf of Guyana's rural poor are motivated by the same kind of socioeconomic handicaps and inequities which lie at the root of McKay's protest dialect poems and which were sufficiently aggravated by the worldwide repercussion of the Great Depression to result in political and labor unrest during the late 1930's and early 1940's. This is the tradition that is shared by Martin's "Ruth," McKay's "Wha fe Do?" and Martin Carter's "University of Hunger." Similarly, poverty and imperial neglect spur on the anticolonial themes of Vere Daly and Walter Lawrence in the early twentieth century, in much the same way that the economic depression of the 1930's sparked the independence movements in West Indian politics and the urgent sense of a national identity and purpose in West Indian literature. The related issues of race and cultural history may just as readily be traced from the background of a Claude McKay who lived and wrote into the postwar period, albeit in a North American setting. Una Marson's "Canefield Blues," for example, and McKay's rural Jamaican themes are explicit enough in the connections that they trace between economic hardship and racial injustice, the same kind of connections that have sparked literary and political protest before and since independence. Although neither the cultural activities of the Harlem Renaissance nor Garvey's Back-to-Africa Movement had a significant impact on the West Indies of the 1920s, it would be wrong-headed to assume that the area was altogether immune to the kinds of sympathies to which Garvey appealed in the United States. As I have already indicated even John E. C. McFarlane felt constrained, in 1923, to take time out from his ethnically placid verse to defend blacks against white racism. In a broadly historically sense, then, the ethnic themes which dominate so much of recent West Indian literature, for better and for worse, react to the racial experience which moved McKay and Marson to protest between 1912 and 1937.

I   *Late Pastoral Verse*

But after these continuities have been duly taken into account, the character and achievements of the postwar period are distinctive. On the whole, this is the period in which the old-fashioned Caribbean pastoral ceases to be the dominant poetic mode. Unfortunately it does not disappear altogether. It flourishes, albeit as a minor tradition, in the bland word-paintings of Jamaican writers like K. E. Ingram, and Carl Rattray. And notwithstanding an erudite bearing of sorts their compatriot, John Figueroa, fails to rise above this kind of mere word-painting in either of his two collec-

tions, *Blue Mountain Peak* and *Love Leaps Here*. In Barbados A.
N. Forde's *Canes by the Roadside* reduces the wordpainting
obsessions of the pastoral mode to its basic absurdities with trite
but aptly captioned pieces like "To a Breadfruit Leaf on My Bed"
or with unabashed imitations of Keats and Shelley in "Sea Bird."
Moreover, one of the inherent drawbacks of the Caribbean pastoral
persists in the works of its more recent devotees: its emphasis on a
rather servile dependence on entrenched (English) literary clichés
fosters secondhand attitudes towards subject matter and to the very
experience of writing poetry. This problem is most noticeable in
the work of John Figueroa, precisely because the reader can sense a
stifled originality underneath the erudite derivativeness of his
nature poems. An occasional work like "The Garden Green and
Great" in *Love Leaps Here* offers direct contact with that originality; but several of the poems in this collection are little more than
adaptations from the classics—"Horace, Odes," "Pastores,"
"Tenebrae," and "Palinurus"—and as such they actually complement that lack of an informing, provocative originality in those
poems which do turn more directly to the Jamaican landscape in
Blue Mountain Peak.

Of course the increasingly minor role of the old Caribbean
pastoral does not mean that the Caribbean landscape loses its
perpetually strong grip on the poetic imagination. If anything, that
grip has become stronger over the years. But there is an important
difference between an earlier preoccupation with a blandly escapist
and derivative word-painting—the Caribbean pastoral—and the
more recent perception of the landscape, not as a background for
neoclassical or neoromantic imitations, but as a living symbol of
the West Indian's historical experience and sense of identity. In
this respect the modern poet has continued the pioneering thrust of
Claude McKay's nature poems by going beyond the vague and
sentimentalized loyalties which suffuse the landscape of much
West Indian poetry up to and including the turn of this century.
But beyond this, the more important landscape poetry of the
postwar period does not only emphasize an original vision of experience as such. It also does this with explicit reference to a strong
sense of a shared West Indian consciousness, one which embraces
but transcends local (territorial or island) identities. This is undoubtedly one of the most distinguishing features of this period. By
contrast McKay, probably the most explicitly West Indian of the
earlier poets, seldom extends his ethnocultural themes beyond

Jamaica in his earlier work; and on the few occasions on which he does this, especially in his North American works, the West Indian framework lacks the precision and intensely conceived dimensions of the West Indian consciousness in the later writers. This West Indian consciousness is not universal in contemporary West Indian poetry. Among the major writers Louise Bennett is first and foremost a Jamaican not only with respect to her folk materials and folk idiom but also on the basis of her social and political perceptions. And in much Guyanese poetry—the works of A. J. Seymour and Wilson Harris, for example—there is a continental dimension in the landscape which enforces the reader's sense of an identifiable Guyanese perspective even when that continental dimension is offered in conjunction with, rather than in opposition to, the idea of a shared West Indian identity. But on balance, postwar West Indian poetry reflects the burgeoning political interest in forging and maintaining cultural and institutional links between the English-language territories of the Caribbean—from the founding of the University of the West Indies to the abortive West Indian Federation of the early 1960's.

II   *Landscape as Experience*

More specifically, landscape poetry reflects this political interest. The landscape is becoming a mirror of the poet's conviction that there is a distinctive West Indian history and identity. Simultaneously, that transformed landscape becomes a West Indian reflection of private feeling and universally shared perceptions. This is the kind of transformed landscape with which Wordsworth McAndrew works in his *Blue Gaulding* collection. The title poem, for example, is a highly imaginative rendering of a typical swamp vignette from McAndrew's Guyanese landscape. It is a vignette of the eternal cycle of life and death and it is centered on the striking figure of the blue gaulding as a bird-angler. The fleeting but vivid image of the bird ("Stilts support the silent, slateblue / Shadow of Patience") merges with the flashing colors and speed of its prey, the creek patina fish ("a shimmering, scaly rainbow . . . streaking for the channel between Life and Death").[1] And that merging both recreates the Guyanese swamp with concrete and lasting clarity and re-enacts the eternal life-death rhythms of experience, within the poet's specific realization of an identifiable West Indian landscape. Few of McAndrew's contemporaries are more explicit than Harold

Telemaque about this kind of landscape poetry. In *Burnt Bush*, a volume which he co-authored with A. M. Clarke and which is pointedly dedicated to "The New West Indian," Telemaque contrasts the "form, style and imagery" of the West Indian's traditional models (English Romantic poetry) with a new emphasis on the cultural dimensions, the West Indian dimensions, of the individual struggle "to achieve the ideal of self."[2] Telemaque does not always eschew what he himself calls the "old jingle" of "the calf's path of the past," particularly in the trite, hackneyed images of his Trinidad landscape in "Little Land" and "Sacrament." But in his better works there is a fresh, transforming vision of his environment. His title poem envisages the lush tropical growth as the affirmation of life after drought. And in "Dowry" the sensuous abundance of the tropical landscape becomes an allegory of the passionate giving of one self to another. The poet's passionate love of his landscape both merges with the celebration of personal feeling and confirms the emotional experience of a West Indian reality.

In more concretely West Indian terms, the peculiar seductiveness of the Caribbean landscape for the West Indian poet projects the poet's vision of a distinctive West Indian heritage and history. Eric Roach, who is better known as a dramatist, provides a notable example of this achievement in "March Trades." The poem is noteworthy on two counts. First, the poet particularizes the Trinidad landscape of his "torrid centre" under the relentless pounding of the trade winds which literally brought West Indian history with them in the persons of Indian settler, European settler and buccaneer, and African slave. The trade winds are now the poetic imagination personified, probing the recesses of the West Indian islands and their sea with a strikingly intense zest for sensory detail and with precise insights into the nature of their history:

> Close eastern windows
> While the high wind blows
> Too wildly in the eaves
> And curtains fill like sails
> And the rooms fret like cabins
> Of gale gripped galleons.
> Make all ship-shape
> In stubborn Colon's simple way,
> In the black slave-trader's way,
> In the buccaneer and pirate way.[3]

Secondly, the poem preserves its intensely West Indian personality while relying heavily on echoes of John Donne ("Earth leans the arctic / Once more to the sun") and of Shelley ("Tossed to the gale / Are driven from the boughs / Leaves ochreous / Of cedar, plum and shrub"). These echoes work very well in a poem of this kind because the use of English literary precedents is not servilely imitative but pointedly functional. The decidedly English referents reinforce the presence of the British heritage in the historical landscape which the poet's imagination now explores. They also impinge upon the frank self-perception of the poetic imagination as a symbol of the historical landscape that it describes; for that imagination is compounded and partakes of all those historical sources—including the British heritage of Donne and Shelley—which have flowed into the West Indian experience. In a clean break from the set formulae of the Caribbean pastoral Roach's imaginative perception of his landscape goes hand in hand with an innovative use of his English literary precedents.

The aesthetic freshness with which Roach handles his historical perception of his landscape is not really matched by Raymond Barrow, but the latter's treatment of his landscape in Belize (formerly British Honduras) reflects a similar disposition towards an informing historical perspective. "Oh I Must Hurry" revels in the lush beauties of the poet's natural surroundings and it projects the poet's fine sense of historical ironies: the very abundance of the unspoiled savannahs inspires an urgent awareness of tomorrow's capacity to ravage the land, just as yesterday's Mayan Indians were destroyed by the followers of that rain-dispensing God who now presides over the present scene of plenty, "capsizing from his open palm / Handfuls of rain-dust, silver and black and gray" (*Caribbean Voices*, II, 88). Even a far less accomplished poem like "There Is A Mystic Splendour" still manages to convey this central irony in Barrow's vision of his landscape: the splendid abundance of life and nature barely masks the deadly violence of the West Indian past. The "mystic splendour" of the poet's dawn-lit beaches affirms the continuity of life, but it is also a reminder of the cruelty, the greed and the exploitation which were inspired by the dubious splendor of the pirate's gold, and which, in turn, have been camouflaged by the spurious romanticism that has historically cloaked the pirate's personality.[4] And in a significant turnabout from the one-dimensional innocence of the old Caribbean pastoral, this kind of landscape is a complex structure of symbols which celebrate the lush tropical vitality while exploring the grim deadliness of tropical history, and which affirms the vitality that has survived, even transcended, that history in the kind of imaginativeness that is represented by the poet's transforming vision.

III   Symbols and Archetypes

Perhaps no single topic in West Indian landscape poetry demonstrates this transforming vision more concisely and with more clarity than does the vulture "John Crow." The bird holds a striking fascination for the West Indian poet, largely because some of the paradoxes of the West Indian's landscape and history seem reduced to their essence in the John Crow figure. It is a thing of incomparable beauty and grace as it soars against the white and blue splendor of the Caribbean sky, yet close up its repulsive features epitomize the grim physical realities of its trade. Even the weakest of the John Crow poems manage to evoke the sense of paradox which surrounds the central image. It is the horror of death loose on the wing above the legendary vitality of the tropical landscape, the kind of horror which is suggested by Jamaica's Carl Rattray ("And Crows Go Circling Round") and Trinidad's Barnabas Ramon-Fortune ("The Crow").[5] R. L. C. McFarlane's "Crow Perch," set in the Jamaican skies, is in a similar vein. But he has a greater sense of the dramatic in presenting the crow's personal impact as a figure of beauty and death and as a grimly symbolic reminder to those who enjoy the pleasures of bed and board.[6] Wordsworth McAndrew's "Legend of the Carrion Crow" is a more effective poem. The bird's ugliness and its role as vulture are counterbalanced by the mystic suggestiveness of its soaring flight, a mystic image that inspired the legend of the bird's successful attempt to penetrate the blue sky in order to "look at the other side"—but at the cost of blackening its body and scarring its face forever in "that sacred blue fire." The legend of the crow is as much a paradox as the bird's conflicting physical images. Having dared to aspire for knowledge beyond its familiar territory, the scarred and blackened vulture inspires a weighty question: "was yours a punishment or a purification?" And that question has immediate relevance for the West Indian who shares the crow's blackness, who has been reviled for that blackness, and who must now perceive the fires of the past, not simply as a cruel and unjust punishment, but also as the source of a new and purposive identity. The John Crow's symbolism is therefore as specifically West Indian as the distinctive Caribbean setting in which it is so deliberately located by the poet: the need to perceive its beauty as well as its ugliness, its vitality as well as its death-functions represents the larger need to comprehend the West Indian experience as a creative process as well as a tragically wasteful history.[7]

On the whole, McAndrew's handling of the John Crow symbol anticipates the complex and disturbing treatment of landscape in the present generation of poets, particularly Anthony McNeill and Dennis Scott. But the John Crow image in McAndrew and his postwar contemporaries is also another symptom of the extent to which the urgent sociocultural climate of that period shapes the poet's perception of the environment. G. A. Hamilton's Jamaican summer, in "That Summer" pointedly replaces the nature-worshipping poet with a new breed of sun-worshipper, the white tourist whose alien presence represents a profitable but culturally enervating relationship for both sides (*Caribbean Voices*, II, 69). Slade Hopkinson's "Guyana: Freedom Year" departs from the ironic statement that characterizes Hamilton's Jamaican beach scenes in order to invest the Guyanese landscape with the political turmoil and hatreds of the immediate pre-independence period:

> Note that the river bed conceals
> Nuggets, and spawn of deadly eels.
> Note too: the selfsame land can feed
> The agouti, and the centipede (*Caribbean Voices*, II, 74).

The landscape themes of writers like Hopkinson are at their best when they are integrated, as in this case, with an art of protest. William S. Arthur's "Shadows on the Canes" exploits the familiar setting of the Barbadian plantation to offer a portrait of the cane-cutter that completely reverses the pastoral escapism of M. J. Chapman's nineteenth-century *Barbadoes:*

> . . . my gnarled
> Twisted limbs, calloused and worn, my hands
> That delved within the muck and mire for strands
> Of broken History.[8]

The symbolic purposiveness of this kind of landscape also lends itself to the ubiquitous island imagery of the nationalist poets. The landscape acquires a West Indian dimension while manifesting its peculiarly insular contours. Islands and sea represent the geographical and political context of a common West Indian history and a shared West Indian sensibility in, say, Eric Roach's "March Trades." But while "March Trades" concentrates on the paradox of a West Indian identity emerging from the destructive past, a poem like Roach's "Love Overgrows A Rock" describes the parallel paradox—that of a shared West Indian consciousness that actually originates with the peculiarly isolated sensibility of an island environment. The endless expanse of surrounding sea enforces the islander's sense of isolation: "My eyot jails the heart." But that very isolation inspires the need for a communal identity that draws upon the common heritage of a shared history:

> So, from my private hillock
> In Atlantic I join cry:
> Come, seine the archipelago;
> Disdain the sea; gather the islands' hills
> Into the blue horizons of our love. (*Caribbean Voices*, II, 216)

Here Roach has invested his archipelago theme with a complex awareness which typifies the handling of the theme by the more sophisticated writers and which obliges his reader to react to the island experience on three, simultaneously perceived levels. The island's well-defined boundaries symbolically enclose the private awareness of the individual, the West Indian archipelago as a whole embraces a specifically West Indian consciousness, and in turn both the private sensibilities of the individual and the collective psyche of the West Indian experience are the symbol and essence of a universal need for human ties ("love") that are as infinite and permanent as the "blue horizons." This theme receives its converse treatment in "I Am the Archipelago." The black West Indian's poverty and colonial subordination are a paradigm of black world history and a symbol of dispossession everywhere. Roach's archipelago archetype represents the divisive history of racial double-consciousness and divided cultural loyalties between black and white, Africa and the West. And simultaneously the archipelago gradually emerges as a whole, rather than a fragment, within which historical divisions are being transformed into a harmonious mosaic.[9]

Roach's archetype also stands at the center of the postwar generation of poems which explore the island dimensions of a West Indian identity. Even the precisely defined national scope of Andrew Salkey's more recent *Jamaica* acknowledges the enclosing, unifying implications of the Caribbean—"our sea"[10] A. L. Hendriks writes very much to Roach's point when he voices a West Indian yearning that reaches out from his Jamaica to the other islands in "To You in St. Lucia."[11] And that West Indian longing coincides with a personal need to experience that contact with others which transcends private isolation. But the tightly organized structure and intense feeling of Roach's poetry is lacking here, as they are in Harold Telemaque's comparable "One People"[12] Ellsworth M. Keane of St. Vincent comes closer to Roach's achievement in the finely crafted "Fragments and Patterns" where the West Indian identity is envisioned as a coherent pattern emerging from the fragments of the past. (*You Better Believe It*, pp. 209 - 213) In "Rhapsody on a Hill" the archipelago symbol describes the West Indian consciousness as part of a pervasive New World sensibility. The poem's language and rhythm celebrate the landscape's seasonal renewal as a rebirth. The poet is the second Noah after the Flood, with "a new world to furnish." This sense of new beginnings is integral to the West Indian's creation of an identity out of the fragments of the past. It is also part of a general New World ethos of renewal and new possibilities. And this is all intrinsic to a universal longing for ideal commitments and cultural reaffirmation:

> And I have stumbled upon
> All the world's wheels and engines
> . . . and someone came running to me
> With the universe
> Like a top spinning in his hands.

In effect Keane has expanded upon the kind of West Indian self-definitions which are at the center of Eric Roach's poetry. These self-definitions now include a New World ethos that joins the private needs and West Indian sensibilities of the Caribbean persona. (*Caribbean Verse*, p. 37).

It is indicative of the rich diversity of techniques and approaches in the postwar period that Andrew Salkey chooses a distinctly non-Western symbol in order to develop the themes which Roach and Keane explore through the Biblical and literary referents of their

Western sources. Salkey's chosen symbol is Anancy, the West Indian version of the West African Anansi. "The World of the Wash
Basin Spider" therefore establishes the conflict between a
transplanted African personality, Anansi the spider-god archetype,
and a hostile new environment—the "slippery white enamel
world" of the West, (*Caribbean Voices*, II, 146). And in "Anancy"
the harmonizing of Africa and the West represents the ideal West
Indian consciousness. As the symbol of that consciousness Anancy
represents an achievement that is at once specifically cultural and
universal: he is simultaneously spider, man, West Indian, and West
African, (*Caribbean Voices*, II, 137 - 138). Taken together the
literary forms of Roach, Keane, and Salkey represent the very
diversity-cum-harmony that they explore in the West Indian
heritage: the forging of an identifiable West Indian identity is complemented by the self-confident handling of the culturally diverse
materials at the disposal of the poet.

Generally, these West Indian definitions stand in a special
relationship with much of the more interesting Guyanese poetry.
The major writers like A. J. Seymour and Martin Carter write unquestionably within the West Indian context of their counterparts
in the islands. But even in their work there is a special Guyanese
dimension that is derived, in part, from their continental rather
than island environment. In the long run, however, this continental
dimension emerges as an analogy of Roach's archipelago symbolism. Among the lesser known writers Frank Dalzell's *Moments
of Leisure* fits in with this Guyanese trait by imbuing his continental landscape with a national consciousness that is essentially the
same as the islanders' ethnocultural perception of the Caribbean
archipelago. In a similar vein Jan Carew's *Streets of Eternity* offers
some effective vignettes of Guyana's continental landscape as the
living symbol of the fragmenting colonial experience specifically,
and the divided human condition in general. In the poem "Atta,"
for example, "precise and ordered green anarchies mapped the
world." Carew who is better known as a novelist is not always as
effective in what is really a very young collection that often suffers
from a gawky style. But in occasional pieces like "Atta" he precisely summarizes the complex body of private, Guyanese, West Indian, New World, universal perspectives. If the lush variety of
Guyana's plains is ironically symbolic of colonial divisions, that
variety is also comparable with the islander's archipelago: it, too, is
a mosaic in which the poet sees a vital diversity evolving from the

fragments of the colonial wasteland.[13] This is the kind of mosaic that Wordsworth McAndrew describes in "Conversation Piece," a poem on the ethnic diversity of Guyana. Notwithstanding the conflicts within and between the ethnic groups, in the final analysis they have to be seen as a diversified entity, as the "conversation piece" of the Guyanese mosaic. Moreover, as a carefully crafted mode of conversation the poem itself represents a unifying harmony, the ideal to which the poet implicitly appeals as he surveys Guyana's historical divisions.

IV   *The Protest Tradition*

The perception of self and group, past and present in the West Indian landscape implies at all times a special interest in the nature of history itself. History is the reminder of a shameful and painful past in one sense: it is the history of the Middle Passage, of slavery and colonization. But in another, more important sense it is a process of perception and becoming. To look closely at the West Indian past is to comprehend simultaneously the fragmentation of the past and the emerging patterns of present and future. In effect, it is to achieve some insight into the nature of time-as-experience in which past, present, and future are juxtaposed continuously. And this insight allows the poet to treat West Indian history as the symbol and essence of the universal experience of time. Keane's "Fragments and Patterns" implies this kind of historical sense, as do works by Roach and others. In Roach's "Archipelago" the black slave of Africa and the New World inspires the moral and cultural resources through which the new West Indian must transcend the enslavement of the past: the archetype is as crucial for the present and future as it is for the understanding of the past. Vera Bell's "Ancestor on the Auction Block" is a somewhat pedestrian version of this theme (*You Better Believe It*, p. 104), but Peter Blackman's *My Song Is for All Men* is more ambitious. In Blackman's long continuous poem the slave archetype personifies not only black enslavement but also different forms of slavery everywhere throughout history. Both in enslavement and in the resulting quest for an untrammeled identity, the Afro-West Indian is a specifically ethnic and universal archetype. The work is therefore a description of the special fitness of the black West Indian to be an archetype of this kind. Here Blackman contributes to the traditional emphasis of West Indian poetry on the need to comprehend ethnic history as an indivisible part of the human experience as a whole. And in this regard *My Song* emphasizes the parallels between diverse cultures in much the same way that Blackman's historical sense grasps the juxtaposition of past, present, and future in the historical continuum.

For a different poetic temperament the tangible continuities of enslavement and oppression engender not only a transcendental vision but also a very special kind of fury, particularly in the distinctively vigorous protest tradition of the Guyanese writers. Martin Carter is the major representative of that tradition, but some of his lesser known compatriots are not altogether insignificant in this respect. In "Guiana's Voice" Frank Dalzell voices a splendidly effective anger at the "legacy" of "empty years." The statement of angry protest is structured with a fine sense of technical form. The initial dawn-setting seems to invite expectations of a pastoral idyll. But instead of the traditional song-birds the pastoral setting echoes to the poet's "full-throated call to action," the call which "bells the sleeping land / To bright-eyed wakefulness." The unexpected voice disrupts the pastoral promise. In turn, that disruption is analogous to the subversive power of the poet's passion and to the disintegrating forces which arouse that anger by virtue of their continuity.[14] Milton Williams' protest poetry is comparable with the passionate sincerity of Dalzell's work, but on the whole he lacks the sense of artistic form and control which makes Dalzell an effective protest poet.

The protest tradition has had to deal with another problem besides that of technical sophistication. The middleclass intellectual's protest on behalf of the underprivileged and the oppressed implies or actually claims an identification with the poor which contrasts with the clear socioeconomic gulf between the world of the poet and that of his subject. The problem is not peculiar to West Indian literature, of course. But it is no less real for all that. Indeed it is sometimes compounded by the even more clear-cut separation between poverty and middleclass comforts in the Caribbean. As I have suggested, McKay's poetry demonstrates how an awareness of this separation inspires the need to establish a certain empathy with the poor and to demonstrate an intellectual connection with the culture of the folk. When he does this convincingly McKay's success has to be traced to the frankness with which he recognizes and analyzes the gulf, exploring his own ambiguous position as intensely as he deplores the disadvantages of the poor.

Not all of McKay's predecessors and successors have achieved his uneven success in this regard. Apart from some of the major writers few have succeeded in the tricky matter of speaking on behalf of the poor without reducing their protest poetry to a sentimental sop of sorts for the middleclass conscience—theirs and their readers'. In the nineteenth century even Egbert Martin's most effective protest work borders at times on a facile heroism and a sentimental gushiness in his treatment of the peasant. In the postwar period William Arthur's pedestrian "Morning in the Village" (*No Idle Winds*) typifies the facile sentimentality that dogs the less accomplished writers who undertake what has become a mandatory pilgrimage to the folk.

But even the more talented A. L. Hendricks is not convincing when he celebrates the strength of a poor peasant woman in "Road to Lacovia:" "bleak earth has brought her close to famine / Yet . . . this woman dares to walk, and sing." (*On this Mountain*, p. 34) This seems all too easy, even facile. There is no demonstrated awareness of the poet's ambiguity as the sympathetic outsider. The political consciousness lacks a redeeming self-criticism. And in the absence of that self-consciousness the work is not so much a moving revelation as it is a condescending gesture. By contrast Eric Roach's "Homestead" is a superior work precisely because of its complex perspective. Without denying the essentially heroic endurance of "slave's son, peasant born / paisan, paisano," the poem confronts and underscores the archetype's experience of numbing poverty. But even more to the point, Roach's dual perception of the peasant as victim and hero is enriched by a penetrating self-awareness with respect to his dual role as sympathizer and outsider. The poet's interest in the peasant is rooted in a link which the poet perceives between them. They are both creators, each in his own way; and the poet's interest in the other's art is supplemented by a frank acknowledgement of the poet's felt need to substantiate, and even legitimize, his art by demonstrating its folk roots. In acknowledging this need he secures a frank basis for his heroic images of the poor: "Poets and artists turn, again; / construct your tapestries / upon the ages of their acres." (*Breaklight*, pp. 98 - 100).

The folk and the disadvantaged are ready-made subjects for the committed art of the protest poet. But they are also attractive because the poet's sense of roots establishes them as the repository of a cultural ethos which is associated with language, music, dance, and lifestyle, and which is attributed to an African heritage or hybrid Afro-West Indian tradition. Moreover those pitfalls which beset the protester's idealization of the poor are also a real danger for those writers who attempt to assume the cultural ethos of the "roots," whatever they might be, by adopting folk idioms. There are a formidable number of these attempts in the postwar period but relatively few successes always excepting of course the special case of Louise Bennett who is discussed in a separate section. Evan Jones' "The Song of the Banana Man" and "The Lament of the Banana Man" are somewhat limited reproductions of the rural Jamaican dialect. They are limited in that although the language is convincing enough, especially when the poems are read aloud, the works as a whole do not really seem to go beyond reproduction for its own sake (*Caribbean Voices*, *I*, 4 - 6, 86 - 87). More recently, Andrew Salkey's *Jamaica* is strongest when his variety of folk idioms (rural dialect, the language and music of the urban Rastafarians, for example) reflects the diverse experiences and visions of Jamaican society as a whole. Holy-roller dance and song represent the cultural duality of Afro-Christian folk religion in Ellsworth Keane's "Shaker Funeral." And in his "Calypso Dancers" the dominant calypso beat which links the dancers in a throbbing mass is, by extension, the symbol of a universal lifeforce.[15] Keane's musical and dance forms therefore both celebrate the distinctive Afro-West Indian duality and the universality of which it is a part.

V   *Calypso and Poetry*

The calypso has perhaps been the single most popular folk form among West Indian poets since the 1940's, though with uneven results. Some poets, like Keane, imitate the calypso form itself. Others prefer to explore the significance of the calypso as a musical tradition in the West Indian experience. Ian McDonald's "Jaffo the Calypsonian" sees the exuberant rhythms and social awareness of the calypsonian's art as a kind of transcendence. The calypso's typical qualities are really a musical version of that historical process through which the West Indian has created an identity and forms that transcend the limitations of West Indian history. Jaffo the calypsonian is therefore the historical West Indian archetype as he creates music and satiric laughter out of his poverty and social disadvantages. His "calypso iron-music" both reflects and transcends the iron-hard rigors of his poverty, and its laughter is

very much like that ironic mask of concealment which McKay discovers in his folk (*Caribbean Voices, II*, 114 - 116). Eric Roach's
"Caribbean Calypso" notes the calypso as the manifestation of a
will to create form and life in the midst of discordance and decay,
but Roach is even more emphatic than McDonald in describing
that will as a pervasive force in the cultural history of the West Indies: the calypsonian's art resembles and re-enacts that intellectual
and spiritual process which enables the West Indian to reclaim a
vital identity and an identifiable culture from the history of the
Middle Passage. And it is typically West Indian in the manner in
which that process of reclamation includes all the discrete sources
of the West Indian past:

> In laboratories of islands, the sun
> Compounds chemicals of cultures, colours, tongues
> Strange everywhere but in their hothouse homes.
> And here the songsmith tunes
> The stiff Shakespearean rime
> To the lilt of Cancer's seas.
> Listen, the lyric drum
> Swings laughter, love and grief
> Through one melodic line. (*Caribbean Voices*, II, 178 - 181).

In short, the laughing mask of the calypso ironically conceals the
art form's complex emotional structure ("laughter, love and
grief"); and in turn that complexity matches the diversity of its
cultural sources. On this basis, the calypsonian's art is identical to
the poetic imagination itself. In exploring the significance of the
calypso, then, poets like McDonald and Roach are really engaged
in a highly self-conscious analysis of the structure and role of their
own art in relation to a perceived West Indian experience. This
self-consciousness demonstrates a new level of maturity in West Indian poetry. The poet is no longer simply writing about a West Indian experience. He is also analyzing the experience and
significance of the creative act itself. In so doing he displays the
kind of artistic self-awareness which McKay brings to bear on his
work; but as the handling of the calypsonian archetype
demonstrates, the postwar poet does so with a surer grasp of the
multiple significance of his Afro-Caribbean folk culture and of its
relationship with contributing cultures. That surer grasp and its
associated self-awareness herald a coming-of-age.

2. Major Writers

I *Arthur J. Seymour*

Among the major poets to emerge during the forties Arthur J. Seymour (better known simply as A. J. Seymour) has been active over a longer period than most. Since 1937 he has published fifteen pamphlet-sized and larger collections of his work and at this time he still remains very active. As a result of this continuous activity his work is anchored both in the postwar generation which saw the emergence of modern West Indian poetry and in the more recent postindependence soul-searching of the 1960's and 1970's. As editor he founded the literary magazine *Kyk-over-al* which was a major local outlet for West Indian writers before the outside world began to "discover" West Indian poetry. He has also been responsible for three major anthologies and for the Miniature Poet Series. That series published individual collections by poets in pamphlet or monograph form during the early 1950's. The publication was undertaken through a small local printery in what was then British Guiana. And in view of Seymour's limited resources the series still remains one of the most ambitious undertakings in the local publication of West Indian literature, particularly when it is appreciated that, for its duration at any rate, the series represented a continuing commitment rather than the sporadic enterprise of an occasional anthology. The publication of Seymour's own collections of poetry also reflects Seymour's entrepreneurial independence: it has been published almost entirely on the author's initiative. Indeed both as editor and poet-publisher Seymour is the foremost example of what has become a Guyanese tradition of sorts, a marked self-sufficiency which encourages writers to publish through their own resources in a minuscule local market without waiting for the profit and usual "respectability" of the foreign publisher. The tradition complements the writers' emphasis on a special Guyanese personality *within* an encompassing West Indian experience, and in the postindependence period it has become part of a general emphasis on self-sufficiency as a criterion of Guyanese nationhood.

Seymour who has lived and worked in Guyana for the most part reflects in his poetry much of the distinctive character of Guyanese writing.[16] He voices the special Guyanese nuances of what he still perceives as a shared West Indian experience. And among the earlier collections, published in the 1940's and 1950's, *Over Guiana*

Clouds and *The Guiana Book* offer the most noteworthy examples of Seymour's Guyanese vision of the West Indian experience. In *Over Guiana Clouds* the familiar continental sense of Guyana's South American setting encourages the usual feelings of limitless possibilities. But at the same time that limitlessness is threatened by the restrictiveness of a colonial past that the poet shares with his island counterparts. Seymour, like those counterparts, envisages the ubiquitous John Crow as the symbol of the paradoxes of promise and restrictiveness, death and creativity, ugliness and beauty, in his Caribbean history. And in this regard his "Carrion Crow" is comparable with, though technically superior to, works by Carl Rattray, Roy L. C. McFarlane, and other contemporaries. While the John Crow represents the paradoxes of Seymour's landscape and history, the diversity of the landscape itself reflects the cultural mosaic of Guyana and the West Indies as a whole. And in "Patterns" as well as the title poem of *Over Guiana Clouds* the historical process which has helped to shape this mosaic is a universally shared, and specifically West Indian, pattern of birth, death, and re-creation.

The Guiana Book collection extends this preoccupation with the historical processes of Guyanese and West Indian culture: the poet's self-consciousness about his own artistic design has been integrated with his perception of a shaping, creative pattern in history itself. "There Runs a Dream" and "Kyk-over-al" are consciously structured with a sense of design that carefully distinguishes the phases of history-as-pattern. That sense of form singles out phases of exploration, piracy, and colonialization which have been woven into the West Indian past, then envisages the kind of new West Indian imagination that will transform that historical pattern into a fresh, creative significance. In both poems and in "Tomorrow Belongs to the People" this transforming imagination is as sociopolitical as it is literary. Seymour's historical sense is integrated with a firm belief in the committed functions of poetry as art. As a committed poet Seymour produces uneven protest art. Protest or commitment as such is not the problem. But, particularly in these earlier collections, themes of historical identity and national purpose are sometimes rendered in a flat, prosaic preachiness rather than in imaginatively designed structures. In works like "Patterns" and "Kyk-over-al" he is effective when he derives his own poetic form from the very historical processes that comprise his theme. However, he seems to be most consistently effective and comfortable with poetic forms that are drawn from

West Indian folklore and folk art, particularly when the folk materials endow his artistic design with a recognizable West Indian framework for his Guyanese motifs.

In "Slaves" the common West Indian heritage finds its voice in the religious folk songs that have come down from slavery:

> Slaves
> Humming in the twilight by the shanty door
> Oh Lord Jesus
> Slaves
> Pouring out heart-music till it run no more
> Oh Lord Jesus (*The Guiana Book*, p. 20)

Seymour has an acute ear for the songs and music of the folk, and he has the ability to transform what he hears into arresting poetry. "Drums," to take another example, successfully relies on the evocative rhythms of the drum to communicate a shared West Indian image of Africa. Similarly, the rhythm of the dancers in "West Indian Dance" is deftly exploited to evoke images of the grotesque and crippling history from which the folk art forms themselves have been created. The dance evokes the African forest on a slave-raider's night, and in the process it reproduces the fearsome African forest that has dominated the self-hating fantasies of an old black psyche:

> You can see the forest-fires and
> the crouched-leaping figures and
> the shadows large and grotesque
> flickering on the trees. (*Selected Poems*, p. 12)

The poem succeeds because Seymour is simply allowing the imaginative vision of his own art to imitate and blend with that of the dancers. And this technique is the more effective in light of the fact that in these folk art poems the West Indian poet emerges as the heir to the folk art tradition of describing and embodying the evolution of a living culture from the past. By way of another example, "Steel Band" stands out from the otherwise nondescript pages of *Black Song*. He has sharply visualized the steel-band players and the instruments which they have literally created from junk (discarded oil drums). The sharply visualized image blends with the band's rhythm to enforce the poet's vision of a creative principle within his cultural history. The steel band becomes a microcosm of that history, by virtue of its music and the manner in which it was created:

> Rooted like crops
> Hammering the tortured steel
> In a rhythmic violence. . . .
> Echoing over the Middle Passage
> Etching these vessels of indignity
> With a profile of sweet sound. (*Black Song*, p. 9)

Both poem and steel band sweep from the memories of slavery (the Middle Passage and the slave plantation "crops") to the harmonizing power of a new awareness.

Seymour's more recent work combines the persistent themes of cultural history with the retrospectiveness of the older man. His memories confirm the familiar patterns of Time's cycles of birth and death, destruction and creation. The West Indies which he contemplates from the vantage point of his age are vigorously new in spirit and in their sense of direction, but these beginnings are themselves part of recurring patterns in which the West Indian created art out of the negation of slavery and affirmed a cultural vitality in the wasteland of the colonial experience. This impression of a constant renewal, of unending re-creation, is pervasive in *Song to Man*. It is also communicated in a highly compact style which is more tightly organized than the frequent wordiness of earlier volumes, and it also suggests the inter-changeability of private and cultural renewals. In "One Name," for example, the mature lover's memories are similar in kind to the recollections of the historical group experience. This heightened awareness of the private experience of cultural history is parallelled by an increasing tendency to treat the human body as symbol. In one of the more recent collections the body is seen repeatedly as an expressive form that is analagous to the poet's artistic design. Here too the preoccupation of the older man is dominant. This is the body-consciousness of middle age. And Seymour exploits the familiar middle-age fears about death and bodily deterioration as a highly expressive medium; for these fears are one way of linking the birth-death patterns of time and cultural history with the creative patterns of art. Hence in the title poem of the *Italic* collection the body writes its own art in the perennial life-and-death series ("Man / Writing his male in the womb"). In this regard it is analogous to the sea

"Writing its scripture on the rock," and to the wind writing "its will in the tree" (*Italic*, p. 7).

In effect, art as expressive symbolic patterns is a universal principle which is mirrored in the body's form and in the recurring cycles of its birth, procreation, aging, death, and rebirth. Hence, to touch another as the poet does in "Handshake" is to hold "the loom of life / Warm in my hand" (*Italic*, p. 12). And on a related level, in "Images Before Easter," the act of introspection is both a private one ("The longest journey is deep / Into one's self") and an allegory of the West Indian's self-exploration: "Each island and each contintent / Has its ground in my being / Everything passes into itself through me" (*Italic*, pp. 15 - 16). Altogether then, this private body-consciousness is intensely introverted. But it is simultaneously the medium for a strongly felt cultural nationalism; and it is as concretely effective as the earlier folk art forms in representing both the private and the national consciousness as distinct but integrated parts of a universal pattern. The intense body-consciousness in the older Seymour is also comparable with the pre-eminence of the private self in the cultural experience of his younger contemporaries—in writers like Derek Walcott and Mervyn Morris who have succeeded the postwar generation. These similarities with both his earlier poetic modes and with his younger contemporaries attest to the essential continuity of Seymour's work. He remains both individualistic and West Indian, in much the same way that his Guyanese experience has been distinctive while merging with the sense of a shared West Indian heritage.

II   *George Campbell*

During the late 1930's and early 1940's, at the same time in which Seymour was publishing his earliest collections of poetry, George Campbell began to attract attention in Jamaica as one of the most politically-oriented of the poets to emerge during the socioeconomic and political unrests of the period. His only collection of poetry, *First Poems* (1945),[17] was published during the most unsettled and promising years of those "times of troubles," years during which Campbell was busy both as poet and political activist. Both on the basis of his political activism and his writings Campbell is the quintessence of the committed protest poet. Language and theme are directed relentlessly by a single-minded dedication to the sociopolitical function of poetry. As a committed poet his work is therefore a direct expression of those tumultuous times. The anger at colonial repression from abroad is matched by an outrage at the social and economic inequities at home. And especially on the latter basis his protest carries on in the tradition of Claude McKay's poetry. In many respects too, Campbell's work exemplifies the weaknesses of protest poetry at its worst and its strengths when it is most effectively executed. As in any protest literature the protest *per se* is not the real source of the aesthetic problem. Rather it is a tendency, particularly in an intense writer like Campbell, to abandon imaginative statement in favor of bald declamation and a crude frontal assault. At the same time, however, his anger and committment are the major sources of his artistic strength. His best writing evinces a vitality and power that are most effective whenever he controls his passion, without diluting it, in order to make room for incisive analysis and complex suggestiveness.

"In the Slums" is a good example of Campbell at his best. The corrosive satire relies on the imaginative incongruities of imagery to reinforce the impression of social inequities:

> In the slums
> Jewel staring eyes
> Of human flies
> Crowd the rims
> Of our social order. (p. 62)

And the jolting image of poverty is followed at the close by a cutting sneer at the comfortable outsiders in "our glass houses." The image of comfortable wealth is both threat and jeer: the "glass" house suggests a fragile security. In "Smells Like Hell" that fragility is masked by a self-satisfied indifference, and the stark contrast between poverty and self-satisfied wealth is underscored by a bare-boned, unmetaphorical style:

> The well fed, well clothed, puffing long cigars
> In comfort roll down in soft padded cars.
> Some men stealing food
> To feed their bellies
> Women breaking stones
> To earn a living. (pp. 59 - 60)

The contrast between a pampered softness and a "breaking" hardness ushers in a skillful blend of statements attributed to the privileged few, some statements sneering at the smelly poor ("The nigger . . . smelled like hell") and others complimenting the speakers on their own self-indulgence ("All lovely, bath salts, steaming water tap").

The racial reference exposes another target. Like McKay, Campbell integrates the ethnic and socioeconomic issues, though in this regard he lacks McKay's complex skills. "Negro Aroused" is merely shrill (p. 28). The black-is-beautiful theme of "Last Queries" is refreshingly direct in its own time, but on the whole its wordiness amounts to a nervous garrulousness that really undermines the theme of racial self-confidence (pp. 29 - 30). "I Was Negro" is more convincing:

> I was Negro: mechanical beast of burden.
> These knotted arms and muscled back
> Have borne loads that my very soul felt,
> And I have struggled on too proud
> To give in. But now, Oh My God,
> I feel tired . . . tired! (p. 31)

There is an impressive control here. The catalog of moods follows the shifts from a mechanical lifelessness in the language, the slow, heavy rhythms of a burdensome condition, the uneven movements of his struggle, and finally, to the colloquial rhythm and energy of the concluding cry of defiance. As usual the passion of the poet's theme has actually been intensified by this kind of control. And on the whole such control is more likely to be found in the angry poems of social satire than in the more idealistic exhortations to racial pride and socialist solidarity. "Democracy" is an unimaginatively preachy vision of the socialist's millenium (p. 65). "Mother" is a sentimental outpouring in which the idealization of blackness is centered on hackneyed images of the black mother as womb and as mother earth (pp. 37 - 38).

Campbell's idealistic poetry is more effective when his subject is the land. In his work the traditional landscape themes owe their immediacy to the peasant's love of land with which Campbell handles his subject. That love is rendered with something akin to intense sexual passion in "We Went Out Into the Moonlight," "I Could Kiss This Place," and "Market Women." In fact Campbell's convincing closeness to the land creates an unusually concrete basis for his nationalistic perception of the landscape and for his heroic images of the peasantry as the symbol of the land and the embodiment of its heritage. Campbell's land is a concretely sensuous and directly emotional experience—much more so than McKay's—and this is the real strength of his better poems about the rural folk. At the same time, however, his dialect poetry is more uniformly ineffective than McKay.'s. "Me An' Me Gal," for example, is a failure that recalls Thomas MacDermot's clumsy attempt to reach the folk through a highly artificial version of their idiom. Generally Campbell is much more readable when he avoids such clumsy imitativeness and sticks to one of the strongest points of his writing—the ability to present his social landscape through the sharply visualized and passionately rendered images of his physical surroundings. This ability is squandered in the emotional and intellectual sloppiness of "Mother," but it is an impressive asset in one of his best poems, "History Makers":

> Women stone breakers
> Hammers and rocks
> Tired child makers
> Haphazard frocks,
> Strong thigh
> Rigid head
> Bent nigh
> Hard white piles
> Of stone. . . .(p. 61)

The precise eye for physical detail is complemented by a nice sense of historical symbolism. As child-bearers and as stone-breakers (for road-surfacing) the women are history-makers in a public, social-building role. Their strength is the power through which a people must create a history of their own from the hard rocks, the "white piles," of slavery and colonialism in the West. This strength and the ethnic pride that it evokes are allowed to manifest themselves in the poem on the basis of a graphic but economical style. There is no facile exaltation of poverty here. Campbell's women are the victims as well as the makers of history. If the rhythmic pounding of the poem's language attests to their steady strength, it also stresses the rocklike hardness of their lot.

This kind of graphic detail also explains the success of the more widely known "Holy." The poem's theme is familiar enough: the cultural diversity of the West Indies and the West Indian's quest for a solid social harmony represent a universal ideal of unity-cum-diversity. This utopian vision is persuasive because Campbell's symbolism depends on precisely detailed description which imparts a sense of realism:

> Holy be the white head of a Negro.
> Sacred be the black flax of a black child
> Holy be
> The golden down
> That will stream in the waves of the winds. . . . (p. 34)

The "white" head of the Black is ambiguous, connoting both age (grey) and the black-white nature of his bicultural identity. The unusual juxtaposition of "flax" and "black" in the next line has a similar effect. And the sonorous tones of the repeated blessing ("Holy . . .") sanction this biculturalism as a positive aspect of the West Indian heritage. In turn, the bicultural West Indies become the symbol of the universal harmony which the poet envisions for all humanity.

Campbell is not usually as persuasive as he is in this poem whenever he attempts to offer his ideal vision of universal unity, a vision that alternates the utopia of socialist solidarity with the utopia of a multiculturally harmonious world. But unconvincing as the explicit statement of his idealism may be in some of his poems, it remains a fact that that very idealism is the shaping force behind the superb realism of his social satire. The fierce protest against racial injustice, socioeconomic inequities, and exploitation is informed by a deep compassion for the poor, a strong Jamaican nationalism that stands at the center of a West Indian experience, ethnic pride, and by a socialist vision of humanity as a whole. Because of the passion with which he espouses his ideals he sometimes lapses into sloppy writing. Whenever he does exercise control the result is the persuasive idealism of "Holy" or the more consistently effective satire of his protest poems. At such times he is impressive, even excellent.

III   *Frank Collymore*

As the founding editor of *Bim* Frank Collymore has earned the reputation of a presiding genius of sorts over postwar West Indian literature. That reputation rests largely on the number of writers who published much of their early work in *Bim*, and on the fact that during the 1950's *Bim* undertook much of the only continuing critical notice of West Indian literature at that time. As both editor and critic Collymore has therefore been responsible for the kind of pioneering enterprise which stimulated the region's literature at a critical period. As a poet his career has been less distinguished. Most of his poetry was written during the 1940's and 1950's. His recurrent themes center on the typical concerns of the period—the landscape, West Indian history, and the social structure.[18] But he develops these themes in most of his work without a really distinguishing style or unique perception. Landscape poems like "In Thankfulness," "Mutability," and "Casuarinas" are actually a throwback to the neoromantic imitativeness of the Caribbean pastoral. He is less derivative in other nature poems like "At Easter" and "Cloud." But despite a less hackneyed style they do not really seem to have a great deal to say.

The historical perception of the West Indian's cultural diversity is handled in a generally unchallenging way in "This Land," but much more imaginatively in "Words Are the Poem." The latter takes the form of a narrative commentary on history, with the poet questioning his relationship with the Middle Passage and its historical consequences:

> What voyage shall he now essay?
> Along the trade routes glide, glimpsing
> New lands old loves? Or peer
> Below the restless surface, discerning,
> Tangled among the seaweed and obscured,
> A shape that might have been a man? (*Collected Poems*, p. 15)

This is one of the relatively few works in which Collymore really demonstrates his strength as poet. He has a real talent for narrative structure, one that allows for the free play of the incisive, yet subtle, irony that is his other strength. The historical narrative that he adopts here unobtrusively develops the usual historical perspective of the West Indian poet—the conjunction of the past and present, the poet as cultural seer, and art as a means of transforming the perception of the past. In so doing Collymore's contemporary poet incarnates, in a *humanized* form, the voyager and slaver of the Middle Passage past. The final query of the poem therefore represents Collymore's irony at its most typical. The mild tone seems innocent enough, reflecting the questing intelligence of the poet as discoverer and interrogator. But the need for the question arises out of those racial myths in (Western) history in which the black slave or his descendant is not assumed to be "a man."

This is the kind of narrative irony which makes "Triptych" one of his better historical poems. Each of the work's three parts describes a specific kind of immigrant to the West Indies—the colonizers and traders, the white indentured servants, and the African slave. All three groups have been brought to the area by the greed of the first. Collymore stirs the reader's revulsion at the white groups and pity for the African "cattle of the slave-ship." But at the same time he unobtrusively compels his reader's acceptance of all three groups as the eternally fused elements of the West Indian identity. Hence each of the three stanzas opens with a refrain that is both a mode of historical perception and an act of acceptance: "I see these ancestors of ours" (*Collected Poems*, p. 32). The poet's historical sense is therefore a form of double vision which compels a double reaction to the ambiguities of the past.

Collymore's ironic subtleties obviously make for a rather different kind of social satire than the impassioned protest of a George Campbell. But in his better poems Collymore is just as effective as Campbell. Where Campbell assaults reader and society with (at his best) a tautly controlled rage, Collymore relies on a finely tuned, almost detached sense of the absurd. "Voici la Plume de mon Oncle," for example, is an excellent satire on the limited and limiting nature of the colonial education system. The facile statement which so often is the undoing of the lesser poet is an effective weapon in Collymore's hands. It imitates the banality of a society and its shallow educational ideals:

> . . . not that they'll be caring particularly who's
> Going to dish out the stuff, or even what it is for that matter,
> Only the platters have to be licked clean,
> And afterwards with the School Certificate nicely framed
> And the New Order hovering suspiciously near the scene! (pp. 92 - 93)

"Roman Holiday" is perhaps the best example of Collymore's comic skill. It is a monologue on a "lovely funeral" by a mourner who eventually discovers that she has been at the wrong funeral all along. But no matter, really:

> . . . it really was a lovely funeral,
> And I don't know when I've cried so much.

And that reminds me, my dear:
Have you heard that his youngest daughter
' Has run away
With the chauffer? p. 90)

"Roman Holiday" exemplifies Collymore's penchant for deflating
social pretentiousness, in much the same way that the
lightheartedness of *Rhymed Ruminations on the Fauna of Barbados*
offers a diversion from the solemnity with which pastoralist and
cultural nationalist alike have treated the West Indian landscape.
In the latter volume as well as in his other comic satires Collymore
displays a capacity to laugh at his art and society, an ability to be
serious without being pompous and to be comic without being flip-
pant. His is the only comic talent of any significance, in standard
English, in West Indian poetry (the comic genius of Louise Bennett
functions exclusively in the folk dialect). Unfortunately for West
Indian poetry relatively little of his work exploits this talent.

IV   Martin Carter

Collymore's capacity for ironic detachment is unlikely in a poet
like Martin Carter who insists on poetry as an intensely committed
art. Individual feeling and social experience are always interlocked
in Carter's work.[19] That interlocking constitutes a pattern of involvement. By implication, the poem's structure imitates that
pattern of involvement and challenges the reader to share the
poet's committment. According to "You Are Involved," "like a
web / is spun the pattern / all are involved" (*Poems of Resistance*,
p. 18). This poem is fairly typical of the tone and feeling of *Poems
of Resistance*, his most substantial collection of poetry.

The political commitment which dominates Carter's poetry is a
direct reflection of his personal career. As a political activist he was
imprisoned by the colonial government during Guyana's turbulent
pre-independence politics of the 1950's. Since independence he has
served in the Guyanese government in a number of roles, including
delegate to the United Nations and Minister of Information. As the
"pattern" imagery of "You Are Involved" demonstrates, Carter's
ethos of involvement goes beyond commitment as such. It is also
based on the belief that experience is really an all-inclusive
wholeness, a universal pattern or web that includes everything. On
this basis the artistic and social commitment of the poet and the

political involvement of the individual are more than a separate
ideological program. In "Till I Collect," for example, political commitment also reaffirms an all-encompassing pattern of wholeness
that reaches from the integrity of the individual and the humane
cohesiveness of society, to the realization of a harmonious universe:

> Over the shining mud the moon is blood
> falling on ocean at the fence of lights—
> My course I set, I give my sail the wind
> to navigate the islands of the stars
> till I collect my scattered skeleton
> till I collect. . . . (pp. 11 - 12)

In the absence of that affirmation the poet's world is one of blood
and "fenced" divisions. Conversely, the ideal of universal
wholeness is implied not only by political commitment as such, but
by the creation of politically committed art.

Altogether Carter's work rests on a compact, tightly woven
dialectic in which the artist's preoccupation with his art and politics
becomes a comprehensive world view. In this respect, of course, he
is comparable with Roach, Seymour, and others who are also
attempting in that same period to place the specifics of West Indian individualism, art, and culture within a humanely inclusive
rather than imperially limited universe. However, Carter's contribution to this tradition is especially noteworthy because both the
lucid compactness of his dialectic and the disciplined economy of
his language have resulted in a body of poetry which, taken
together, represents the very kind of interlocking or unity that he
envisions. Moreover he evinces a self-discipline and a facility for innovative imagery which ensure the kind of protest art that stands
well above wordy, run-of-the-mill protest verse. In "I Clench My
Fist," for example, the confrontation between the colonizer and the
colonial is the allegory of a divided universe. The poet's reaction,
as artist-activist, to this fragmentation suggests a compacted
wholeness ("I clench my fist") as well as a harmonizing power ("I
sing my song of freedom"). The gestures both demonstrate his own
rage and promise a compact and harmonizing sense of wholeness
(pp. 14 - 15). This progression from an image of fragmentation to a
vision of wholeness represents the thematic pattern of Carter's most
important works—"Cartman of Dayclean," "This Is a Dark Time
My Love," "Death of a Slave," and the famous "University of
Hunger."

Interestingly, Carter's ideological activism re-enacts the same movement from fragmentation to pattern which dominates the cultural analysis of writers like Ellsworth Keane. On the whole, then, the tight thematic context of Carter's work enables any one poem to become a microcosm of his poetry. But, from another point of view, this becomes a limitation as well as a strength. His single-minded emphasis on political commitment as wholeness results in technically polished and generally competent writing but his emotional range and appeal are limited. Here too, the problem is not one of protest poetry as such. In Carter's case the problem arises from a failure to develop sociopolitical themes except within a tightly organized schema. That schema confers an effective wholeness, but in the final analysis it deprives Carter's work of the complex range, even the vital untidiness, of protest artists like Claude McKay and even George Campbell.

V   *Wilson Harris*

In 1951 A. J. Seymour's Miniature Poet Series published some of Carter's early poetry as *The Hill of Fire*. That same year also saw the publication of Wilson Harris' first poetry collection, issued in the Miniature Poet Series as *Fetish* under the pseudonym Kona Wartuck. Since then Wilson Harris has done most of his work in the novel form, but his second volume of poetry, *Eternity to Season*, published three years after the first, demonstrates that he is also a poet of some substance. *Fetish* is pretentious rather than substantial, due largely to metaphoric excesses that make for a turgid, unreadable style. *Eternity to Season* is much better written on the whole, but it too suffers from the old excesses in spots.[20] It seems that Harris himself is aware of this fault since in a recent reprint of the collection he has excised some of the troublesome verbiage. But a recurrent drawback is not simply verbiage as such but also a matter of feeling. There is a flood of carefully devised images which sometimes fail to communicate the kind of intellectual and emotional pressure that would justify such an abundance. In works like "The Beggar Is King" this lack of justification results in a pompous incongruity between subject (the impoverished Guyanese laborer) and the obvious, rather obtrusive convolutions of Harris' imagery. Curiously enough, Harris at his metaphoric worst is not distracting (in the tradition of most poets who suffer from the same affliction) but simply monotonous. In "Rice," for example, the relentless succession of metaphoric elaborations and convoluted statements creates its own peculiar sameness. In his generally enthusiastic introduction to *Eternity to Season* Seymour diplomatically describes Harris' shortcoming as "the way the beauty of the imagery is overlaid by the flux of philosophical correlation" (p. 5). But even at its worst Harris' style challenges the reader's understanding and, not least of all, patience because it always promises the insights of what is clearly a powerful and wide-ranging imagination.

The dramatic poem "Canje," set in a rural Guyanese village, is awkwardly executed throughout with a great deal of excessive writing. But Harris' general drift is always arresting. Anticipating Derek Walcott's *Another Life* by nearly twenty years, Harris' poem examines the lives of his folk through the archetypes of Greek myth—Ulysses, Tiresias, Achilles, and so forth. The objective conforms with the bicultural dimensions within which Harris and others perceive the West Indian experience. The Greco-Guyanese myth-heroes embody the duality of the Guyanese experience; and more specifically, the poet-seer Tiresias now represents the Guyanese poet as the essence and analyst of that duality: the bisexual image of Tiresias symbolizes the bicultural identity of the poet, his imagination, and his folk.

Indeed, quite apart from the artistically limited "Canje" *Eternity to Season* is populated by the archetypes of Greek mythology (Agamemnon, Antaeus, Prometheus, Laocoon, Ulysses, Calypso, Achilles, Anticleia, and Heracles). The figures represent a wide range of symbolic insights into the Guyanese, and West Indian experience. Anticleia, in the poem of the same name, becomes the slave-mother, in "Heracles" the title hero is the slave, and in "Teiresias" the legendary seer embodies the poetic vision of history and universe within a specifically West Indian context. Concurrently, Harris is using these archetypal roots of Greco-Roman and Western culture as a means of exploring the cultural roots of the West Indies: the very concept and use of archetypes are based on a preoccupation with a sense of roots. Moreover, the archetypal mode is used to explore time-as-experience. The archetype is the creation of the past, a symbol and function of the links between past and present, and accordingly, the poet's perspective on the cultural history of his own world. Hence in "Teiresias" the poet-as-seer represents the ability to perceive the future in the present, just as the "Teiresias" archetype himself embodies a continuity between the (Greco-Roman) past and the (Afro-West Indian) present:

> The subtle links of time
> bind this dark village: the old slave lanes, the broken road,
> the dense groves sheltering shady trees, symbols
> of time past and gone. (p. 24)

Slavery in its different forms establishes a continuity in West Indian history, and on this basis the West Indian experience of time fits in with the archetypal representation of time as the continuous flow and intermingling of past, present, and future. In effect, the history of West Indian slavery becomes an allegory of a continuing, universal enslavement to history itself.

"Teiresias" is one of those rare poems in which Harris sustains an ease and a directness of statement without lapsing into strangling verbiage. And this achievement may be of special significance since Tiresias as poet and seer represents the clarity of a fully aware perception of history and the role of the artist. Indeed a fully aware self-perception promises freedom from the chains (self-hate, colonialism, and so forth) of the past. Freedom in "Achilles" is therefore a progressive, unrestricted movement through time. As the "great runner" the Achilles archetype embodies that kind of mobility, and as the voyager his is the "re-discovery that time is the oar of life." This kind of mobility bespeaks a purposiveness that transforms time from a mere enslavement to history, to a vital sense of direction and identity. As in the works of his contemporaries, Harris' individual, West Indian, and poet all come together as a collective imagination with a special significance for the West Indian and with universal implications: "Time is no fixed boat or inevitable doom / but is the motion of men and matter in space, subtly / flowing and binding into universal action, into construction" (p. 27).

On the whole "Achilles" is another well written poem displaying the kind of discipline which allows Harris to blend his archetypal symbolism (mobility, power, creativity) into his central theme with economy and precision. This is also true of "Creation" in which the abstraction of Harris' theme (creation itself as freedom and infinite power) is developed without undue flourish in a succession of clearly defined and concrete images. First, that familiar Guyanese sense

of an infinite landscape lends itself easily to the grasp of creation as
an infinite, universal force, a "unity of extremes that reach from
one end of the world / to the other." Second, it is an "immensity
of greatest power" that is symbolized by that ocean which links
Harris' continent with the West Indian islander's perennial consciousness of the sea. Thirdly, it is represented by the "strips of
coast" that are Guyana itself with its Afro-West Indian capacity to
survive and transcend the Middle Passage past through a "celebration of spirit." And fourthly, to complete the pattern of increasingly specialized, or microcosmic examples, creation is the individual
spirit itself (p. 47). The pattern of the poem progresses inward from
the perception of a universal macrocosm to the individual as
microcosm. As such it represents a kind of focusing. It is therefore
an aesthetic confirmation of Harris' emphasis on perception as
movement and on creation as an endless, infinite movement. In
poems like these Harris' craftsmanship is superb, and the clarity of
vision is unsurpassed. After this volume of poetry he turns to prose
fiction, producing a series of some of the most distinguished novels
in West Indian literature. But even on its own and despite its undeniable shortcomings *Eternity to Season* represents a major contribution to the West Indian poet's exploration of time and history
in the Caribbean experience.

VI *Philip Sherlock*

Philip Sherlock's work is substantially less in quantity than that
of his major contemporaries. But he offers a relatively wider range
of feeling than someone like Wilson Harris who, even at his best,
remains as a cool, detached intelligence that seems incapable of
warm involvement or untidy passion. Sherlock too is an alumnus of
Seymour's Miniature Poet Series. His *Ten Poems*, which was
published in that series, is his only collection, but he has since
published work in a number of literary magazines.[21] He has worked
as historian (co-authoring two studies of West Indian history),
educator (high-school teacher, vice-Chancellor of the University of
the West Indies, and most recently secretary-general of the
Association of Caribbean Universities), and as the collector of West
Indian folktales. And these varied interests have clearly sharpened
his interest as poet in the problems of defining and communicating
a West Indian consciousness (he was already fifty-one years old
when *Ten Poems* appeared in 1953).

"A Beauty Too of Twisted Trees" endows the landscape with the kind of historical and cultural significance that is standard in the literature of the postwar generation. The surprising beauty and vitality of the death-like tree are an allegorical comment on the course of West Indian history: "The harsh insistence of the wind / Writes lines of loveliness within / The being of this tortured trunk." But the work also evinces the understated but very real emotional power with which Sherlock endows his intellectual perception of the West Indian experience. This is also true of his perception of the poet's role within that experience. The wind metaphor is therefore centered on the function of the poetic imagination in shaping a West Indian consciousness. The Biblical and literary allusions which follow elaborate on this role. The persistence of life and beauty in the death-like tree is analogous to the water flowing from Moses' rock and it contrasts with the absolute sterility of T. S. Eliot's wasteland in "The Hollow Men." Moreover the deathliness of what really turns out to be a tree of life is compared with the life-in-death symbolism of the Crucifixion and the Hanging Man in Eliot's *Wasteland*.

Allusions of this kind are more than thematic analogies. They also demonstrate the imaginative process through which the poet transforms the twisted tree into a symbolic tree of life. The allusive structure performs the usual role of establishing the poet's ambiguity: he is adopting the tools of his Western heritage to articulate his hybrid West Indian self-definitions. And like the ambiguous John Crow of other West Indian poets Sherlock's tree is symptomatic of the historical affirmation of life and beauty in the unlikely setting of West Indian history. This is all familiar enough. But Sherlock handles his familiar themes with a distinctive tone and style. The highly allusive structure is combined with a diction that is simple, even lean at times, and strongly affective without being crudely emotionalistic. The entire poem presents its central and unifying symbol, the tree, as a self-revealing phenomenon rather than as baldly explicit statement. The symbolic connections with West Indian history are allowed to suggest themselves to Sherlock's reader through the accumulative effect of his imagery rather than by way of a sledge-hammering emphasis.

This kind of imagery suggests a talented eye for precise, highly evocative detail. And the language which conveys this detail confirms that the poet has a keen ear for effective diction. The understated but strong emotional appeal of his style is derived from

the measured and deliberate emphasis of statement: "A beauty too
of twisted trees . . . [their] record proud of strife, of life" (p. 12).
This is the kind of unobtrusive and deliberately measured style that
makes "Jamaican Fisherman" one of his most impressive works:

> He stood beside the old canoe which lay
> Upon the beach; swept up within his arms
> The broken nets and careless lounged away
> Towards his hut beneath the ragged palms.
> Nor knew how fiercely spoke his body then
> Of ancient wealth and freeborn regal men. (p. 9)

The "broken nets" and "ragged palms" emphasize a dislocating
poverty that is nicely counterbalanced by the fisherman's
"careless" stride. That carelessness is two-fold: it implies the for-
titude which enables the fisherman to cope with his poverty, but
even more to the point, it underscores the differences between the
poet and his subject. The fisherman's "indifference" to his poverty
and to the alleged splendors of his African past is presented, not as
fact, but as the poet's assumption. It is the poet who assumes that
the fisherman is indifferent to his poverty; and it is the poet who
really cares so much about the African heritage. In effect, Sherlock
offers an unreservedly realistic portrait of his fisherman's poverty
while managing to project the idealistic, even romanticizing, implications of the poet's perception of his subject.

Sherlock's strength lies in his ability to see the West Indian's
poverty as it really is, to recognize the cultural losses caused by the
historical break with Africa, and at the same time, to demonstrate
the manner in which those losses have encouraged the artist to sen-
timentalize the folk and the African past. Moreover, in stripping
away the middleclass sentimentality with which the folk archetype
has often been treated, Sherlock emphasizes the real, as opposed to
attributed, dignity and beauty of his folk. In the sonnet form of
"Jamaican Fisherman" the typically measured tread of Sherlock's
language matches the man's self-confident stride. The careful
attention to detail impresses Sherlock's reader with a sense of artistic form that complements the fisherman's physical power and
beauty:

> Across the sand I saw a black man stride
> To fetch his fishing gear and broken things
> And silently that splendid body cried
> Its proud descent from ancient chiefs and kings.

The poem's rhythmic and visual images of the fisherman's presence confirm his very real, rather than romanticized dignity. But, to complete the complex patterns of Sherlock's themes, even the attributed dignity eventually assumes a nonromantic function: the poet's dreams of an African splendor become an allegory of the fisherman's splendid vitality and of his own inherent dignity; and notwithstanding the facile, sentimental uses to which the African heritage may be put, the affirmation that such a heritage exists remains crucial both for the poet who voices that affirmation and for the fisherman who is, sadly, indifferent to it.

These are the kinds of complex insights which Sherlock brings to bear on his themes of West Indian identity in his work. They are the insights that stand at the center of much of the best West Indian poetry in the post-war period. At their best the poets are able, as Sherlock does in "Jamaican Fisherman," to project both their detachment from and involvement with the folk. At their worst they can be guilty of a sentimental condescension and facilely revolutionist notions about their Afro-Caribbean nationalism. On both counts these poets are anything but unique. Their successes and failures are integral to their exploration of their evolving cultural consciousness. And that exploration, together with its attendant pitfalls and triumphs, has been inherited by a later generation of writers.

CHAPTER 4

The Oral Tradition:
Sparrow and Louise Bennett

O NE important effect of the national movement in West Indian literature has been a heightened awareness of the fundamental importance of oral traditions in the vitality and continuity of the region's culture and art. Increasingly, critics as well as the writers themselves have been emphasizing the importance of these traditions, not merely as the source for the writers but also as significant art forms in their own right. In this regard we have moved from the folkloric enthusiasms of Walter Jekyll's collection of Jamaican work songs and folk tales, at the turn of the century,[1] and from the adaptation of Jamaican folk forms in the uneven dialect mode of Claude McKay's earlier works. The current emphasis is on the essential integrity of the folk art which has been sustained by the oral tradition—in music, poetry, and tales. Concurrent with this increasing emphasis on the oral tradition of folk poetry, there are various projects aimed at collecting the formidable wealth of oral materials throughout the region. In some respects these efforts are in a race against time, judging by Olive Lewin's recent prognosis on behalf of the Jamaican Folk Music Research Project: "Every day an old Jamaican dies, taking with him stores of wisdom and knowledge of our past which will be lost to us forever. Every day outside influences increase. So every day our task becomes more difficult, more urgent."[2] But although the collection and the orderly collating of West Indian folk literature remains a continuing and incomplete undertaking, it is nonetheless possible at this time to take the measure of the essential significance of the oral tradition in poetry by looking in some detail at two of its major forms, the calypso and the oral poem in dialect—or more specifically, the calypso art of "Sparrow" Slinger Francisco (Grenada and Trinidad) and the comic genius of Louise Bennett's Jamaican dialect poetry.

As composers and as performers Sparrow and Bennett conceive of their oral art in terms which Edward Brathwaite for one has traced back to the African slaves' use of their new Western language and to the slaves' creation of art forms within that language: "It was in language that the slave was perhaps most successfully imprisoned by his master; and it was in his (mis-) use of it that he most effectively rebelled. Within the folk tradition, language was (and is) a creative act in itself; the word was held to contain a secret power"[3] Brathwaite's point is well taken, particularly in the light of Walter Jekyll's outsider's reaction to the Jamaican folk and their art. The "dusky" Jamaicans whose music and tales charmed Jekyll impressed him with "their many good qualities, among which is to be reckoned that supreme virtue, *Cheerfulness.*" Conversely, this one-dimensional image of the folk goes together with a fairly limited perception of their oral art as "an appropriate accompaniment to the joyous labour of this sunny, happy land" (*Jamaican Song and Story,* pp.liii, 6). By a curious irony of literary history Jekyll is the perfect example of that white buccra who revels in the "joyous labour" of the black peasant and who is pilloried by Quashie's sarcasms in the dialect poetry of Jekyll's young protégé, Claude McKay. The "(mis-) use" of buccra's language by Quashie and his actual counterparts in the oral tradition has been covertly subversive. What has come down as the image of the grinning, compliant slave or the perennially joyous peasant is often a grinning mask which disguises a complexity of feeling and perception—including a quiet subversion of the buccra's establishment. As McKay clearly recognizes in his better dialect poetry the laughter of work songs is often mocking rather than complacent, and the dance may be less a celebration than an expression of pain. The grinning mask of the oral tradition therefore represents a deeply ingrained irony that goes back to the original rebellion of the African slave through the Westerner's language. This is the kind of irony to which George Lamming alludes in his remarks on the West Indian's use of laughter: "West Indians are in the habit of laughing at every goddam thing" (*The Pleasures of Exile*, p. 90). Or in the words of an old Jamaican axiom, "You tek bad somet'ing mek laugh." And this too is the irony that informs the art of calypsonians like Sparrow.

I *Sparrow*

Like most calypsonians Sparrow has a wide range of themes: sexual intrigue, politics, poverty, racial relationships, among others. The polymetric structure of his songs is combined with the steady, infectious rhythms of the calypso form to suggest a lighthearted celebration.[4] But in the sexual themes of a work like "Lulu" that lightheartedness really masks a serious purpose. The lover's erotic plea ("Let's spread some joy") is conventional enough, and so is the transparent hypocrisy of Lulu's coy refusal:

> Ah'm afraid you make a calypso o' me
> Ah know nobody goin' see, an' is only the two o' we
> Sparrow Ah 'fraid you goin' make a calypso o' me.

Lulu's rather obvious eagerness to "spread joy" has been checked by the fear of the calypsonian's notorious practice of converting private as well as public lives into objects of ridicule.

But looked at more closely, this is all more than a trite lover's plea to his coy mistress. It is also a serious examination of the calypsonian's function in society. More precisely, Sparrow appears to question the painful, sometimes brutal process, through which the calypsonian fulfills the role of political commentator, satirist, or social critic. The calypsonian's "word of honour," like the passionate lover's pledge of secrecy (or like Lulu's chastity) may be fragile, even imaginary. And like the more conventional journalist whose shoes he often occupies, the calypsonian is in constant danger of blurring the faint line between the "honour" of fair criticism and the banality of mere scandal-mongering. In effect, the bawdy rollicking style and the highly conventional situation of "Lulu" disguise the double-edged irony with which Sparrow develops his themes of social criticism and artistic self-scrutiny: the double standards and the hyprocrisies of public morality (represented here by Lulu's moral pretentions) are juxtaposed with the moral ambiguity of satire in general, and of the calypso in particular. The grinning mask of the carefree lecher becomes the medium for the calypsonian's self-appraisal.

In "Congo Man" the ironic mask explores a racial theme by way of the ever-present sexual motif. Superficially, the song appears to reinforce the standard Western notions about the cannibalistic "savages" of the "dark" continent:

> Two White women travellin' through Africa
> Fin' themselves in the hands of a cannibal headhunter.
> He cook up one an' he eat one raw
> They tas'e so good he wanted more. . . .
>> I envy the Congo Man
>> I wish I coulda go an' shake he han'
>> He eat until he stomach upset,
>> An' I . . . I never eat a white meat yet!

And when the repeated "white meat" references make the (interracial) sexual motif unmistakable, it would seem at first glance that Sparrow has merely reproduced the stereotype of the white goddess' black stud. But it is really difficult to miss the satiric implications of laughter in the song, especially when the singer reproduces and mocks the Congo Man's lecherously expectant chuckles:

> An' when the water was warm she started to wiggle
> The Congo Man started to laugh an' giggle
> Ha! ha! ha! kla! kla! kla!

For the sheer exaggeration of that laughter is itself suggestive. The Congo Man is an object of ridicule, not as an African reality, but as a Western image of the black male and of Africans in general: Africans are savages and cannibals, and black men have an insatiable lust for white women. The animal sounds of the Congo man's laughter therefore underscore the very real savagery of ethnosexual myths about blacks. At the same time the exaggeration invokes a sense of the horrific, and in so doing, the singer recreates the atmosphere of paranoia, the nightmarish sense of insecurity, which have engendered the ethnosexual image of the black stud.

But here too Sparrow's irony is characteristically double-edged, for it is also directed at the victims of that ethnosexual image—at the white woman who perceives the black male only as stud and at the black man who is obsessed with white women as "white meat." The Congo Man therefore embodies a widespread obsession which has infected even the singer himself ("I envy the Congo Man"). And the singer's envy incites a feverish curiosity ("Peepin' through the bushes to see what's takin' place") which suggestively places both himself and his audience in the roles of voyeurs. Consequently the Congo Man is really enacting a symbolic ritual on behalf of the singer and like-minded members of his audience: the black male's desire-hatred for the white woman, as object of sexual craving and racial revenge, is dramatized by the sadistic overtones of the cannibal motif; and on her side, the white woman's loathing for, and fear of, the savage cannibal actually reinforces a certain yearning for the forbidden. Apparent resistance ("wiggle") and cries of supplication ("beg") have actually become acts of excited participation.

These themes are not original. They are even rather *deja vu*. But for that very reason they are a measure of Sparrow's considerable gifts as a performer, and as a judge of performance-as-commentary: the familiar themes have been blended into a performance that is actually a symbolic ritual. The Congo Man's sexual rites are not simply a statement about a well-known, frequently documented experience: they also involve the singer and his audience in a disturbingly personal way in that experience, forcing the latter to perceive it not simply from the comfortable detachment of the moral analyst or the social critic, but with the voyeur's uneasy yet excited involvement. The grinning mask has been transformed into a masquerade, into the kind of ritual group experience which symbolically involves the singer's subject, the singer himself, his audience, and by extension his society at large.

Transformations of this kind are central to the kind of calypsonian performance that Sparrow's art exemplifies so well. The performance of a private experience places that experience in the public domain; the individual perception or statement becomes a symbolic ritual with implications for the community at large, in much the same way that the carnival masquerade envelopes the entire community. Consequently in a work like "Monica" the singer embellishes the story of individual hardship and poverty until it becomes an unobtrusive re-enactment of all that is grimly familiar in West Indian poverty:

> The she say to me
> "Sparrow Ah think Ah makin' a baby
> But Ah don't know
> Who is the father or who to give it to."
> She want me to help she out
> But Ah planning to back out
> So Ah turn 'round an' ask she flat
> What she think she husband go say 'bout that.
>   So she tell me:

> "Me ain' know me dear
> The man he ain' care
> This mister does leave me here alone
> For weeks he don' come home
> I have to depen'
> On me seaman frien'
> When me seaman frien'
> Bring they frien'
> Is then Ah have cash to spen'."

The insistent rhythm of the calypso's structure, together with the sexually exploitive energies of the singer all have the effect of projecting that familiar mask of joyous celebration. But here too the joyous mask barely conceals a disturbing reality. Monica's predicament is both a crushingly private one and a symbol of her social environment. Here too the calypsonian's ego as performer has deliberately disturbing implications for his audience: by frankly inserting himself into the woman's story ("Sparrow Ah think . . . ") the performer becomes the living symbol that connects Monica with the audience. Her predicament represents theirs. And by a similar extension of roles, his cold-blooded detachment from her difficulties ("Ah planning to back out") is not only a kind of self-defensive reflex (after all Monica is as economically calculating as he is sexually exploitive) but it is also a mocking imitation of the calypsonian's audience in its smug detachment from the poverty and inequities which involve them all.

Altogether the involving or enveloping effects of Sparrow's art arises directly from the fact that like all superior calypsonians he is conscious of the essential orality of his art form. That is, he is aware of the extent to which his calypso medium is an oral performance in which the respective roles of singer, subject, and audience are distinctive entities behind appropriate masks (detachment, coyness, pathos, lechery, and joyousness) as well as interwoven parts in a continuous, symbolic masquerade. At the same time Sparrow's art offers analogies to the literate structures of those poets who transfer aspects of the oral folk tradition to their written work. Hence as a transparent disguise for pathos or pungent realism Sparrow's grinning mask recalls the deceptive light-heartedness and ambiguous vitality of Claude McKay's personae in the dialect poems. But considerable as has been Sparrow's achievement as an artist in the oral tradition of the calypso it is Louise Bennett who remains as the unquestionably supreme artist in any oral medium in the West Indies.

She clearly surpasses any of the poets who attempt to transfer the dialect mode of the oral folk tradition to the written page, largely because she chooses to work within, rather than merely with, the oral tradition of folk poetry as a vital art form in its own right. And as performer she evinces the ability to offer an unmatched range of feeling and insights all of which are embodied by a large collection of personae who assume a full-bloodied reality in the poems, largely because Bennett's remarkable self-discipline as artist allows them to function on their own with a minimum of authorial obtrusiveness.

II   *Louise Bennett*

The significance of the performer's role in Sparrow's calypso art is the direct outcome of the fact that Sparrow is after all a professional artist who, like all calypsonians, is as much performer as he is composer. In the case of Louise Bennett that performer's role has its source in her relatively early involvement in the theater. Hence during the late 1940's she studied at the Royal Academy of Dramatic Art, then worked with several repertory companies in England before returning to teach drama in Jamaica. As both performer and composer she is comparable with the calypsonian in that she relies less on the explicit statement about the ironic deception of the grinning mask, and more on the suggestive contrast between diction and rhythm, on the one hand, and on the other hand, the implications of her themes. But when she does offer explicit statement it does shed very useful light on the ironic import of those rhetorical devices which she and other artists in the oral tradition exploit.

Her most important, and comprehensive, collection of poems, *Jamaica Labrish*, offers several examples of such explicit statements.[5] In "War-Time Grocery," composed during the Second World War, the scarcity of food gives rise to the warning that "happy" talk and laughter among frustrated shoppers are definitely deceptive. And in "My Dream" the political unrest of those hard times and the resulting pressures for independence feed a discontent which is barely disguised: "Dog a-sweat but long hair hide i' / Mout a laugh, but heart aleap!" (p. 156). The witty, trenchant proverbs drawn from the colloquial language of the folk both explain and exemplify the idea of a mask. The proverb in "My Dream" is comparable in this regard with the very similar technique of "Dutty Tough" where wartime hardships persist, despite appearances to the contrary, like the dry toughness of rock-hard dirt in drought: "River flood but water scarce yaw, / Rain a-fall but dutty tuff!" (p. 20). And in proverbs like these Louise Bennett, like McKay before her, discovers the precise, built-in antitheses through which the folk verbalize their sense of conflict and social contradictions, and which the poet adopts as a ready-made mode of ironic statement.

But in developing the ironic implications of the performer's grinning mask Bennett goes beyond explicit statements of this kind. She also relies on the evocative contrast between her subject matter and her *manner* of statement. In "Dutty Tough" the elaboration on hard times lends itself to a raucous liveliness, even to farcical embellishment:

> Saltfish gawn up! mackerel gawn up!
> Pork an beef gawn up same way,
> An wen rice an butter ready,
> Dem jus go pon holiday! (p. 21)

Altogether then, the playful raucousness of a Bennett poem is based on the same tactic which informs the calypsonian's irony—the traditional function of laughter and play as disguise and resistance in the language of the folk.

As I have already suggested, this is the same tactic which McKay discovers in his adoption of the folk idiom. But Bennett is far more effective in adopting this tactic, and consequently far more effective as a folk ironist, than is McKay. McKay is highly conscious of the *literate* medium of his poetry, even when he writes dialect poetry. And, as already pointed out, both the successes and failures of his dialect work derive in part from his attempts to reconcile the orality of his sources with the frankly Western implications of his sense of a literary heritage. On the other hand, Bennett has not had to wrestle with this felt need to reconcile her poetry, as Jamaican oral art, with a perception of her poetry as an extension of an English literary tradition. In the first place her superior talent is complemented by a surer grasp of the aptness and integrity of the oral forms themselves, a grasp which is partly an aesthetic counterpart to the growing national self-confidence in the period during which she writes. Secondly, like the calypsonian, she is deliberately and consistently aware of her role as poet-performer: as performer

108 WEST INDIAN POETRY

in the oral tradition she is immersed in the modes of rhetoric and perception that are enclosed by that tradition. And that immersion results in a much more consistent and convincing handling of her folk materials.

Indeed Bennett does not hesitate to emphasize the orality of her art and her own role as performer. She has performed much of her work on radio and at arts festivals in Europe and North America as well as in the Caribbean; and a major proportion of her poetry actually appeared for the first time on her radio shows since the 1940's. Consequently publication has really been an after-thought, of sorts, in terms of her function and achievement as an artist in an oral medium. Her emphasis on the oral nature of her medium is clear enough in "War-Time Grocery" with its reference to the persona's laughter-and-talk as masks. In "Boo" the scathing satire on an arrogant politico who is indignant at being booed rests on the special appeal (and effectiveness) of booing in a society in which oral modes excite a certain zest. And by extension, the poet's identification with the booing mob transforms her political satire into a "boo" of sorts. As the title of "Kas-Kas" suggests, the poem is another work in which the poet deliberately presents her art as an oral statement. Here the title announces that the work is not only about talk as such, but is actually an exercise in scandal-mongering. The poem itself evokes the sounds and interpersonal complications of the communal texture of the oral tradition:

> I hear say Jane sey Imo sey
> Dat Amy sey dat Sue
> Tell smaddy dat Miss Matty sey
> She hear sey Sam beat Lou. (p. 187)

Bennett's emphasis on her oral milieu is often accompanied by a subversive slyness regarding the hallowed world of print. When the local newspaper heralds the overflow of the city reservoir ("Overflow") Miss Lou is outraged by the absurdity of it all: the dam which is supposed to counter the effects of drought is dry when her garden needs water and is only full when her garden is already overflowing with rain. And, adding insult to injury, the newspaper's gratuitous report smacks of the absurd superfluities which seem endemic to the great world of print, its unresponsive technological culture, and its uselessly full reservoirs. Moreover, that annoying superfluity is mockingly echoed by the flood of Miss Lou's own sense of her orality:

> Write newspaper meck dem know!
> Tell dem sey I sey fe sey is not
> De dam one overflow! (p. 46).

In this bold irreverence for the printed word Bennett affirms the integrity of her oral mode and the cultural perspectives that it represents. Hence the newly enfranchised voter who is delighted to discover her name on the voters' lists ("Votin' Lis' ") still refuses to be overawed by the legendary magic of the printed word. And the dance motif with which she celebrates her individuality appropriately reinforces the nonliterate criteria of her oral folk culture:

> Ah gwine mek dem tan deh beg me,
> Ah gwine mek dem tan deh pine,
> Ah gwine rag an haul an pull dem
> So till ah mek up me mine. (pp. 133 - 134)

Here the self-expressive individualism of the oral mode has been integrated with the sociopolitical freedom that is represented by the choices of the ballot-box (the poem was written in the 1940's to mark the granting of adult suffrage).

Bennett's affirmation of the oral tradition and her accompanying satire on the world of print are also in response to the traditional middleclass phobias which assume that the Jamaican dialect is necessarily inferior to standard English. "Bans O' Killing" is a spirited counterattack on those who would "kill" or eradicate the use of dialect, and it is also a pointed reminder that in the large linguistic scheme of things English itself is another dialect, neither inferior nor superior to its Jamaican counterpart. Indeed if she imputes limitations to any language form, she appears to do this in a work like "Dam Overflow" where she underscores the limited modes of perception that seem to be inherent in the literate view of things and people. And more explicitly, "Mash Flat" questions the general usefulness of a narrowly standard application of English to a society that is as hybrid in its sources and structure as is Jamaica. What Bennett appears to be suggesting here, both by direct statement and by rhetorical demonstration, is that the Jamaican's dialects (standard and folk) represent different modes of perception that can only be effectively communicated through the respective languages and that, conversely, middleclass snobbery against the folk language really denies an integral part of the Jamaican identity.

This claim is made in these poems with an assurance and clarity
that are striking in the still unclear atmosphere of the early independence movement. It is this kind of claim that gives a forceful
point to the mockingly outrageous suggestion in "Jamaica Ant'em"
that the anthem of the new nation be based on traditional folk songs
rather than on the usual neocolonial borrowings from the mother
country. And the prejudices against which she directs her satire also
explain the import, and impact, of two of her most notorious poems,
"Votin' Lis'" and "Rightful Way." The playful disdain of the
printed word in the first poem is informed by the typical hyperboles
of the oral mode. In promising to vote, she undertakes not only to
make the usual "X" but "wat me cross out gawn like storm." The
poem provoked a furor, largely because it was feared that the un-
educated and inexperienced voter would take that last statement
literally. Consequently Bennett obligingly offers a corrective in
"Rightful Way" in which the proper voting methods are explained.
But she does this with a characteristic tongue-in-cheek demeanor.
Her self-recriminations for possibly misleading her unlettered fans
barely conceals a hearty contempt for those who confuse nonliteracy
with literal simple-mindedness; and, conversely, she raises very
serious questions about the ability of the world of print and standard English to grasp the subtleties and innuendoes that underlie the
decidedly robust language of the oral mode.

In the light of all this it seems clear that Bennett's use of dialect is
more than a blandly self-serving display. For quite apart from the
functions of folk irony and the satire against literate middleclass
modes, she is highlighting the various nuances of the oral tradition
in order to immerse her audience in the experience of the folk
themselves, ranging from the touching tenderness and expectations
of "Mass Wedding" to the raucous invectives of quarreling women
in "Cuss-Cuss." Moreover, this kind of immersion is more than that
traditional middleclass pilgrimage to forgotten folk roots, or the
"outcast's" customary search for lost cultural sources. More to the
point, this all involves the searching analysis of the specific function
of language as oral technique in her characters' lives. In "Cuss-
Cuss," for example, the elaborate, far-fetched metaphor which
ridicules an adversary's foot has a specific function:

> Yuh foot shapeless an lang
> Like smaddy stan far fling dem awn
> An meck dem heng awn wrang. (p. 189)

The most immediate object is ridicule. But it is also the kind of ridicule which, for the purposes of the verbal battle, must demonstrate a formidable skill with language, with images that are formidable precisely because they have the tone and impact of instant coinages. In effect, language becomes a substitute for physical violence (as it actually does in this poem) because it carries with it a violence of its own, and because its flow and energy display an awesome imaginative power. In this sense the personal quarrel is a kind of one-up-womanship in language. And the violent functions of language in a personal encounter of this kind are an extension of the aggressiveness and of the self-defensive masks which Afro-West Indian culture has devised since slavery from both its Western and non-Western sources.

Thus the metaphoric structure of Bennett's poetry is actually an imitation or reflection of the essential creativeness of the unlettered folk's sophisticated use of language. This explains why so little, if any, of her "topical" materials are ever dated. The wartime poems, for example, are as fresh and as striking as when they were first performed because by virtue of their style their focus is less on the specific topics of the 1940's (food shortages, high prices, the war itself) and more on the continuing modes of perception and communication which they dramatize. The comic personification of clothes ("Soap Vacation") and rice ("Rice Gawn") is a case in point. So are the abusive similes which the street peddler culls from those ubiquitous front-line reports in order to hector reluctant customers. In "South Parade Peddler," for example, the speaker vents her frustrations on a succession of unfortunates who are: as ugly as a demolished Graff Spe,[6] as toothless as a torpedoed boat; and as bald as the aftermath of an "Hair-raid" (p. 27). This is also a two-way process. For if the war in Europe supplies grist for local Jamaican concerns, the war itself is also reduced to its essential obscenity by being subjected to the outrageously irreverent puns of the non-literate whose style reflects an acute understanding of European language and civilization. In "Perplex," for example, the speaker professes to be confused by it all, comprehending only that that madman Hitler had appropriately called himself a "Naasy" (that is, "nasty" and "Nazi"). Clearly the European's wars have been seized upon to dramatize another continuing conflict—that between black identity and the Westerner's Eurocentric notions of culture and civilization. Thus that age-old self-defense by blacks in a white world—the feigned inability to understand the other's language—is also a form of subversiveness, particularly when the Europeans' internecine (as well as interracial) violence raises questions about the humaneness of their vaunted civilization. Therefore in "Italy Fall" the speaker's puckish refusal to "understand" the jargon of wartime ideology ends up as a reflection on the European's sickness, and the Jamaican's sagacity: having been identified as "Socialis," "Fasis," and "Axis," the Italians may very well be on the way to becoming "pendecitis." The highly suggestive disease motif reaches its inevitable resolution in the contemptuous dismissal of both Germany and Italy at the end of the poem: "Ef you fly wid John Crow, yuh / Wi haffe nyam dead meat" (p. 104). The proverb is familiar enough in the folk language (If you fly with the vulture John Crow, you will have to eat carrion). Having compared Italy and Germany with carrion and vulture, the proverb both pinpoints the European's human failings and affirms the moral insight and humanity of the despised black experience; for that Twi derivative, "nyam" (from "enãm") echoes and celebrates the speaker's West African sources at the same time that it turns the familiar charges of cannibalism against the traditional accuser—the European.

Given the immediate significance of talk and oral style in the lives of Bennett's speakers it follows that they are acutely sensitive to the function or dysfunction of the outsider's language. "Distinguish 'Merican," written to welcome the late Adlai Stevenson on a 1955 visit to Jamaica, seizes upon an example of dysfunction in order to underscore Bennett's social satire. The irony of having an American launch a "Buy Jamaican" drive on behalf of local industries has obviously not escaped the poet. The visitor's oratory and intentions are laudable enough, but the essentially absurd context of his talk is emphasized by the telltale deafness of a bystander and by the half-admiring, half-irreverent summation by her friend: "Words, words, dem deh is words, / Is pure words dem a-chat" (p. 158). Words, especially the "big" words of standard English are not incomprehensible to the folk. Bennett's characters are all able to function inside as well as outside standard English whenever they feel the need to do so. But big words are always suspect whenever they are used for their own sake. Whenever this happens they attract the scorn of the Bennett speaker whose language is so firmly rooted in the functionalism of style. And Bennett's satire is intensified in the face of language which is not only absurdly nonfunctional, but actually becomes part of a mechanical, unresponsive process which exacerbates human suffering. "Poor Gum" is therefore a scathing attack on a useless and long-winded conference on racism (in Great Britain), in which the comical sufferings of the big-talker's gums are wryly analogous to the real hardships that the conference is supposed to solve.

Here again we are brought face to face with a certain uneasiness about the intellectual and moral limitations of a narrowly middleclass, exclusively literate perception of the black West Indian experience. This uneasiness does not flow from a rejection of Western culture and literacy as such. Indeed Bennett can be aggressively pro-Western in due season. But it does suggest that she perceives the West Indian personality in dual terms. Consequently a narrowly literate or Western mode of self-perception would not only be snobbish for the West Indian; it would also be a kind of cultural suicide. On the other hand Bennett handles her oral folk medium as a bicultural rather than exclusively non-Western form. For in addition to its Africanisms the dialect of her speakers is constantly interacting with the standard forms, imitating and subverting them in turn ("Perplex"), or creating its own structures from the substance of the printed word ("Nazi") perceived orally ("nasty") rather than visually. Hence quite apart from the fact that McKay's artistic development was more deliberately literate (and therefore more problematic for his dialect techniques), Bennett is never really constrained to follow her predecessor's questionable experiments with dialect-standard compromises. She is far more assured than he is of the cultural *inclusiveness* of the folk idiom. This assurance, together with her complete immersion in the idiom itself, also explains her consistent success in subordinating any standard technique to the design of her oral form: her rhyme schemes, for example, are never as incongruous or as obtrusive as they are in McKay and others.

Altogether then, the distrust of a narrowly intellectual wordiness must be traced to the duality which Bennett perceives in her folk traditions. And if her oral mode encourages a distrust of pretentious literacy, the converse is also true: the folk's admiration of, and loyalty to, a Western middleclass ethic of achievement encourages a frank admiration for foreign "twang" and for "big words" used in a certain way. Hence in "Amy Son" the success of Amy's son abroad is measured by his overseas "twang" as well as by his material achievements. By a similar token foreign language or twang is absurd, even annoying, when it comes without the impressive substance of material achievement—in much the same way that "big words" are rejected when they lack human understanding. On the whole the strong nationalism of an unaffected Jamaican "patois" is counterbalanced by the frankly middleclass aspirations of Bennett's Jamaican poor. And the double irony of "Noh Lickle Twang" summarizes this duality very well. The young man who returns from the United States with money but without even a little "twang" is something of a disappointment. For if language without substance is an absurdity, a man of substance without a matching language, or dress, is something of a family disgrace.

On the whole this kind of ambiguity lies at the root of some unevenness, even inconsistencies, which Bennett's poetry reflects when it touches upon the very notion of a national consciousness in the Jamaican and West Indian experience. Hence the victory celebrations at the end of the Second World War lend themselves to a nicely balanced irony. In the light of the West Indian's wartime hardships, and in view of the Nazis' "nasty" racial image, Bennett's close identification with the victorious allies ("Victory") is not merely a colonial loyalty but a rather pointed declaration of the Jamaican's self-worth. But some poems are marked by a striking colonial loyalty, or by an absence of the anticolonial rancor which appears in contemporary writers like George Campbell. "Duty Bound," for example, expresses a popular fondness for a departing colonial governor without really questioning the symbolic significance of the colonial governor's office. But, in turn, this indifference to the imperial presence contrasts with the spirited attack on British colonialism in "My Dream," written in 1949, eight years before "Duty Bound." This apparent shift in viewpoint is really analogous to the ambiguity of "300 Chrismus," a work in which Bennett joins in one of the more dubious exercises of West Indian colonial history—Jamaica's *celebration* of three centuries of British rule. On one level the poem does join the celebration on the occasion of the tercentenary Christmas, and in this vein it chides those who would cheapen the significance of the moment through sheer overabundance and triviality:

> T'ree hundred bargain sale an
> Tercentenary parade,
> Tercentenary John Cunoo dance,
> T'ree hundred masquerade! (p. 77)

But on another level, beneath that overt complaint, the choice of language implies a subversive view of the tercentenary itself as a memorial to the continuing masquerade and the cheapening ("bargain sale") effects of the colonial experience.

The point is not that Bennett's poetic vision is itself insincere or hopelessly inconsistent. More pertinently, as a highly disciplined artist she subordinates the authorial voice completely to the cultural personality and values described by her art. Hence the primary function of her art is to reproduce in all its self-revealing details, the Jamaican's national consciousness as it shifts and varies from one Jamaican to another, or as it wavers within any single individual. The aim is not to offer an overview of a collective consciousness deduced from her cultural ambience, or even created by the poet herself. Instead the objective is to portray a variety of attitudes among her wide collection of personalities, and to express the contradictions, self-conflicts and uncertainties within any single personality. And in doing this the artist consistently allows free rein to her speaker. She is far less likely than an Edward Brathwaite, for example, to move both outside and inside her characters and their folk milieu, both celebrating their heroic endurance within and raising critical questions from without.

Throughout all of this she does leave her audience with a very strong impression of the essential ambiguities of a national consciousness either in Jamaican society as a whole, or in the behavior of the individual personality. "Strike Day," written during the turbulent 1940's, reflects the burgeoning racial and national pride of its times: "Nayga was a-reign teday / An wite man got a fall!" (p. 116). The voice of protest here is as striking as it is in the "My Dream" of the same period, but in turn it clearly contrasts with the imperial loyalties of "Duty Bound." And in "Colonisation in Reverse" the rambunctious Jamaican self-esteem is skilfully interwoven with a pointed self-criticism to create an impressively ambiguous image of the poet's subject. History has been reversed by the mass migration of Jamaicans and other colonials to the capital of empire during the 1950's and early 1960's. The former seat of empire is now being colonized. And thanks to Great Britain's generous welfare system Jamaican migrants are now reversing the age-old relationship of imperial exploiter and colonial victim: Jamaicans are taking bread from their English hosts. But on the other hand, colonization in reverse involves some questionable Jamaican conduct, an exploitiveness that makes no distinction between the imperial "enemy" and other Jamaicans.

Once again, these ambiguities or inconsistencies may be traced not so much to Bennett herself as to the world whose viewpoints she reproduces with a ruthless eye, and ear, for authenticity. If there is an inconsistency or puzzling lack of clarity in her voice, if she seems to move from one position to another (on the issue of Jamaican nationhood versus West Indian federalism, for example), her audience always needs to remember that her voice has been subordinated to the personality that it describes; and that in this regard her art comes as close as art ever can to a kind of objectified reality. Her poetic voice fascinates and challenges her audience precisely because her characters seem to be so irrefutably independent of a controlling artistic vision or authorial judgment. This partly explains the fact that the woman's experience which so clearly dominates her work remains, paradoxically, unobtrusive rather than explicitly reiterated—particularly when she is compared with someone like Una Marson. In Marson the voice of overt protest inevitably compels a specially alerted attention. In Bennett the preoccupation with the Jamaican woman's situation is even more pervasive. Indeed no other West Indian writer has dealt at greater length with the West Indian woman. And in no other writer has the world of the Jamaican (and the West Indies as a whole) been presented almost exclusively through the eyes of women, especially the rural women and the poorer women of the city. But notwithstanding all this, Bennett's poetry illuminates the woman's own situation with a minimum of direct commentary. And such commentary as does appear is presented, as usual, as the viewpoint of a fictional character. On the whole the straightforward moral indignation of a Una Marson is absent, even in works which bear the burden of protest statement: "De A. T. S." slyly attacks the old sexual double standard by urging the legitimacy of the woman's frank sexual initiative; "Solja Work" and "White Pickney" jeer at the racial attitudes which lead light-skinned women into sexual partnerships with white soldiers; and both "Bans O' Woman" and "Registration" celebrate the opportunity to consolidate the political and social power of women through the founding of the Jamaican Federation of Women in the 1940's. Generally, Bennett eschews characters who make direct statements about the woman's situation, and instead allows her women to offer indirectly revealing, sometimes contradictory, levels of awareness about their sociosexual condition.

Each woman's overview of her own situation is integrated with her personality. The speaker in "De A.T.S." attacks the male double standard by cherishing marriage almost as a kind of revenge, a device to possess and hold a man for the sake of possession; and this limited awareness of her role as woman has to be distinguished from the more straightforward celebration of women's power, or potential women's power as full-fledged individuals in "Registration" and "Bans O' Woman." In effect Bennett is concentrating on the presentation of a succession of various viewpoints, in that manner in which she handles the issue of national consciousness. The enthusiastic feminist from North America is not likely to find a completely untrammelled notion of woman's liberation in these poems that would compare closely with a "radical" American feminism: Bennett's relentless realism leaves no room for visionary women of the revolutionist's tomorrow—no more than it leaves room for clear-cut, uncompromised visions of a Jamaican or West Indian consciousness. Instead the women whom she describes are variously militant, conventional, strong, weak, and more often than not, a combination of these qualities. In this respect they are analogous to the ambiguities and self-conflicts which they themselves reveal, as Bennett's ubiquitous spokeswomen, in the national experience as a whole. They are therefore, in a very special way, the very incarnation of Bennett's poetic truth.

CHAPTER 5

The Personal Odyssey of
Derek Walcott

IN a 1949 issue of *Bim* magazine Frank Collymore published an introductory essay on the poetry of Derek Walcott.[1] The essay which describes the precocious achievements of the then nineteen-year-old poet is appropriate in more ways than one. As the editor of *Bim* and as a popularly acclaimed father-figure of sorts of contemporary West Indian literature, it seems only fitting that Collymore should be one of the earliest critics to offer public recognition of what has become one of the truly major talents in the literature. Furthermore, Walcott's achievements as playwright and poet are a culmination of the intellectual energies and the cultural self-searching of Collymore's generation. Walcott's poetry is, in many respects, a continuation of some of the most fundamental themes that dominate postwar West Indian poetry—the separate-but-communal implications of the archipelago archetype, the West Indian artist as symbol of the West Indian's history of cultural creation, the uniquely Caribbean as well as significantly universal dimensions of that cultural history, and the vital role of folk art in giving expression to all of these. Walcott's major contribution to these literary traditions has been the uniquely personal dimension within which he develops his poetic vision: the West Indian experience appears in his work through the intense feelings and complex vision of the poet's persona, and through that persona Walcott's reader experiences Walcott's world on a dramatically individual, even private, basis. Finally, in view of the fact that *Bim* offered such substantial support to new writers trying to publish their work locally, it is only fitting that the first critical introduction to Walcott's work should appear in *Bim:* after all Walcott not only published much of his earliest work in *Bim* and similar magazines, but he also elected to remain in the Caribbean at a time (the 1950's and early 1960's) when it was unusual for a major writer to do so.

The year of Collymore's essay was also the year in which the first two collections of Walcott's poetry were published as *25 Poems* and *Epitaph for the Young* through a small printery in Kingston, Jamaica. These were followed four years later by *Poems*. These early volumes show the considerable artistic talents and anticipate the major themes of his more mature writing, but they suffer on the whole from a baldly didactic approach and from an immature wordiness. What emerges in his subsequent poetry is that increasingly personalized vision which provides his work with a complex and unifying individuality. His is an intensely private vision of the West Indian's experience as individual, New World archetype, and universal symbol. The evolution of this vision is best observed in his four major collections of poetry, *In a Green Night, The Castaway, The Gulf,* and *Another Life*[2] (a fifth volume, *Selected Poems,* consists of reprints).

I   In a Green Night

The first of these volumes, *In a Green Night,* is a very convenient introduction to Walcott's major poetry because in it the reader can clearly distinguish the major themes which he shares with his postwar predecessors and which gradually merge, through the subsequent volumes, to become the complex personality through whom the poet perceives the West Indian experience. In view of this gradual fusion, it is not surprising to find that the major themes of *Green Night* are not only distinctive as such but are also organically related to each other. Appropriately enough the first poem, "Preludes," introduces one of those major themes—the island consciousness which is derived from the pervasive presence of the sea, and its historical implication vis-à-vis the Middle Passage, and which is as central to Walcott's identity themes as it is in comparable West Indian poets before him. To see the "variegated fists of clouds" over his island, and to watch the ships dividing the horizon is to be sharply reminded of his island identity, especially when he finds himself in the "blue reflection" in the eyes of visiting tourists. The circumscribed dimensions of his island are joined with the limiting identity which the tourist imposes upon the "native" islander, and together they impress the poet with a sense of insignificance. But at the same moment he is well aware that his poetry is a mode of affirming his real humanity, of allowing him to transcend the limiting impressions of his island identity. The poet's personal awareness as islander and the significance of his art are therefore interchangeable: his island identity is measured (that is, circumscribed in space and by socioeconomic boundaries), but it is also capable of a boundless self-affirmation; and in this regard it is analogous to the poet's art, disciplined and measured, but affirmative and transcendental. On the basis of this analogy, his private self becomes a public metaphor. Or, in the more negative language of the poem, his life "must not be made public / Until I have learnt to suffer / In accurate iambics" (p. 11). The stage has been set for the personal odyssey which gives an individual immediacy to the exploration of the islander's identity.

The personalized vision is crucial. Walcott is distrustful of the outsider's limited, and limiting, perception in diaries, travelogues, and tourist posters. This distrust which he voices in "Islands" is actually an updated version of the continuing postwar rebellion against the perspectives of the Caribbean pastoral and it is the converse of the commitment to a highly personalized experience of the island identity. In the words of the poem, "islands can only exist / If we have loved in them" (p. 77). In other words, to experience the islands is to comprehend the complexity of the islander's sense of individuality; and conversely, it is also to be reminded that all human beings are essentially islands who persist in remaining distinctive, even separate, despite the sensation of universal affinities and notwithstanding the more immediate, more concrete, pressures of a racial or group consciousness. The island identity is therefore rooted in the paradox of a cherished separateness and a strong need to merge with the other. "A Map of the Antilles" explores this paradox, one which had already become a major theme in postwar poetry and to which Walcott lends his typically individualized approach. Thus it is the Odysseus archetype who appears in this poem, symbolizing a passionate search for meaning and community but confronted at the same time with the realization that there is a "raging sea between each bed"—that the "dangerous currents of dividing grief" are strong enough to "make our union a mockery of the heart" (p. 55). "A Careful Passion" develops the paradox on a more personal level, replacing the familiar Odysseus figure with those of two lovers. Their private, sexual relationship is analogous to the paradoxes of the islander's experience: the conviction of their essential separation from each other is deep, but that conviction is counterbalanced by their need for each other. In turn, that need reflects their sense of a shared humanity, and in more specifically West Indian terms, a supportive, national consciousness. Accordingly, sexual intimacy, or its promise, is offset in the poem by the "original curse" of Cain's children, the curse of loneliness and isolation (p. 44).

This theme of isolation is characteristic of much of Walcott's poetry, and it distinguishes his perception of the West Indian's island identity from that of most major West Indian poets. For while Walcott too participates in the celebration of a West Indian consciousness that has evolved from an unlikely history and from an insular separateness, his much greater emphasis on the persistence of individual separation tempers his perception of a communal or regional identity. In Walcott's poetry people *are* islands unto themselves, notwithstanding the long-lived axiom to the contrary. On the whole his poetry is less likely to celebrate some easy, transcendent nationalism or ethnicity, and more likely to become a painstaking, often painful, analysis of the personal tensions that are generated between the conflicting pressures of group and individuality, between the moral and emotional promise of a communally perceived ideal and the human failings which blunt that promise. And in *Green Night* it is the poet's vision of the United States and the New World which links the isolation theme with the theme of betrayed ideals. When Walcott looks at the United States from within, as a visitor, he does so with a heightened sense of the promise and failure of the American's New World vision. In "Fragments and Epitaphs" a Central Park statue seems to re-enact the promise of life and new beginnings out of a historical fragmentation—in the manner of Ellsworth Keane's "Fragments and Patterns." But the statue's stoniness reminds the poet of an American incongruity: the fact that "The Muse hath a stone breast in America" overturns the American's cherished New World ethos of spiritual vitality and a creative humaneness. But the West Indian too is involved in the petrification of a New World ideal. The poet's final gesture to the statue is therefore self-incriminating as well as accusatory: "I rest dark hands thereon and pray for peace" (p. 50). On the one hand, the touch of the poet's hands expresses the need to come together in a shared ideal within a revitalized New World experience. But, on the other hand, it is the gesture of one who is an accessory to the commercialism of America's stone-hearted Muse: his hands beg for a "piece of the action."

The failure of love and idealism in Walcott's New World are especially acute on two counts. First, unlike the ambivalence of
Claude McKay's outcast West Indian, Walcott's West Indian is
totally identified with the New World as his inherited and natural
ambience. And this greater involvement with the New World,
which Walcott shares with contemporaries like Keane and Eric
Roach, results in a proportionately intense experience of the New
World's failure. Secondly, that failure is the more striking when
measured against the mythic process by which the expectations of
the New World have been promulgated, especially in the United
States. Consequently one of the incisive ironies in Walcott's perception of the New World mystique is the fact that the history of the
New World has often been an extension rather than rejection of Old
World failures. In "Ruins of a Great House" black slavery in the
New World dramatizes the failure of the vaunted humanism of New
World beginnings. The New World morality has been disappoint-
ingly Old World, notwithstanding the New World ideal. The rotting relics of slavery recall the European's sin: "the abuse / of ignorance by Bible and by sword." But they are also reminders that
America has also contributed to this extension of Old World values
into the New World. The ruins of a West Indian great house are
comparable, not only with the marble of Greece, but also with
"Faulkner's south in stone." And, by extension, the poem as a
whole explores the New World as an Old World ruin. Consequently, the great house is not only a plantation artifact of the Americas,
it is also the European's empire: it is crowded with the ghosts of imperial "heroes" like John Hawkins, one of the first British slavetraders, and rotting with the "leprosy of Empire."

If the West Indian's experience of New World failure is intrinsic
to a New World identity, then by a similar token that identity also
partakes of Old World sources. On this latter level "Ruins of a Great
House" is a poem of discovery in which the New World West Indian gradually uncovers his Old World sources. Those sources are
negative: they are symbolized by slavery and colonialism. But in a
more positive sense they include the poet's own literary heritage:
hence his eyes "burned from the ashen prose of Donne" as he gazes
at the great house. Appropriately enough this gradual uncovering is
an extended metaphorical digging into the ruins, beginning with
the outsider's detached gaze of disapproval and moral superiority,
then passing on to a growing identification with the slave-ancestors
who, like the "moth-like" white girls of the mansion, are now rot-

ting in the ground before the poet, and finally on to an acceptance of both slave and master as intrinsic parts of his present totality. That kind of acceptance is the basis on which Walcott's West Indian self-perception has to be distinguished from Claude McKay's. McKay is the perpetual outcast, acknowledging and grasping both his Western and non-Western selves, but remaining perpetually ambivalent towards both. And that continuous ambivalence is the source of the imaginative tension in much of McKay's work. In Walcott, on the other hand, ambivalence or unresolved self-conflict is the starting-point, and the poetry itself becomes an experience, often a painfully intense one, of resolving the personal crisis of identity by reconciling the diverse elements of his West Indian personality, no matter how disparate or irreconcilable those elements may seem. In this regard the development of themes in "Ruins of a Great House" is not simply the process of unearthing New World and Old World sources. It is also a clearly defined experience, a highly personal one, in which the poet progresses from moral disapproval and racial anger at the ruins and the rot that have been bequeathed to his present world by the history of empire and enslavement.

As he digs into the significance of the ruins, moral indignation, racial resentment, and a sense of cultural malaise are all tempered by a growing compassion: the British, too, were once slaves, not only to the Romans but also to the moral turpitude which made it possible for them to have been slave-masters; and in the light of the poet's ties with both slave and slave-owner the ruined great house now appears "as if a manor of thy friends" (pp. 19 - 20). Here compassion is more than an act of sympathy for the black and white slaves of the past. More importantly, it is an act of self-acceptance since it involves the sources and symbols of the poet's own hybrid cultural personality. This kind of compassion therefore evinces the capacity to affirm a sense of moral purpose and cultural vitality in the face of the New World's moral wasteland. And that affirmation, so typical of contemporary West Indian poetry, places Walcott's act of self-acceptance within a characteristically West Indian context: he has not only reconciled the distinctive features of his New World and his Old World, he has also integrated his private self-awareness with a West Indian consciousness.

But to pass on to yet another, related theme of *In A Green Night*, what of the African presence in this compassionately realized West Indian experience? On the whole Africa is subject to very much the

124   WEST INDIAN POETRY

same kind of struggle which moves from a painful insecurity
(alienation and attraction) to a hard-won degree of self-acceptance.
"A Far Cry from Africa" is repelled by both the barbaric colonizer
and the violent rebellion of the African; the poet is paralyzed by the
feeling that he is "poisoned" with the blood of both sides (p. 18).
But in the final analysis this paralysis gives way to the realization
that he is the product of both sides. There is nothing easy or facile
about that realization. For here as in his subsequent works Walcott
is sensitive to the pain as well as triumph of accepting *all* the
sources of his West Indian heritage. The acceptance does not negate
or minimize the guilt of slavery and colonial violence. Total acceptance of this kind involves, not an easy transcendence or triumph,
but a realistic awareness of his own complex identity. In other
words, the poet's own complexity is a personalized symbol of the
West Indian's diversified *wholeness*, incorporating a New World
and an Old World and integrating a European heritage with the
Africanisms of an Afro-West Indian culture. Consequently, the
frank loyalty to the English language and its heritage in "A Far Cry
from Africa" is complemented by the dialect of "Parang." In a
similar vein language reflects the cultural diversity of the West Indian in "Sea-Chantey" and "Pocomania." In the former work
(p. 66) the poet's language relies on the music and imagery of
Western Christianity and on the Western folk art of the sea-chantey
structure to describe "the litany of islands" and the "rosary" of the
Caribbean archipelago. On the other hand, "Pocomania" relies on
language that is heavily accented by the rhythm of island dialect,
and the religious theme combines the Christian archetypes ("The
Lamb," "The Host") with the African religious symbol of the
gourd; the "shepherd" who presides over the pocomania worship is
both the representative of the Christian Shepherd and the prac-
titioner of rites that go back, like the gourd, to a West African past;
the "host" is both Holy Ghost and ancestral spirit in the African
sense, and if the goat-skin drum which greets the Host has a distinctive West Indian appearance its religious function evokes the role of
the elephant-skin drum in Akan ritual (p. 35). Finally those
language forms and those cultural symbols which emphasize the
West Indian's duality are brought together in "Tales of the
Islands." On the one hand the British "correctness" of the "Ox-
bridge" (Oxford and Cambridge) graduate describes the traditional
calypso carnival from a distinctively Western and "outsider" viewpoint; and on the other hand, the celebration is described through a

local folk idiom which reproduces the polymetric structure of the calypso and immerses Walcott's reader in the language and sounds of the "fête" itself:

> They lead sheep to the rivulet with a drum,
> Dancing with absolutely natural grace
> Remembered from the dark past. . . .
> Poopa, da' was a fête! I mean it had
> Free rum free whiskey and some fellars beating
> Pan from one of them band in Trinidad. (p. 28)

Those echoes of the calypsonian's art brings up the final major theme of *In a Green Night,* one which brings all the others together. It is the familiar postwar preoccupation with the role of art as a process which offers a sense of shape and unity in the West Indian experience, as a creative experience in which the poet represents all West Indians in their historical reclamation of a culture from the rot of the colonial heritage. Consequently the folk art of the calypso (like the art of Sparrow or Louise Bennett) brings together the diverse sources of the West Indian heritage (English tongue, Afro-Caribbean music and language, and peasant roots). But once again Walcott reworks the standard West Indian theme within a specifically individual context. His reader is always aware of the poet's personality, not simply as an abstracted archetypal role, but more immediately as a concrete personality groping towards a sense of cultural wholeness and artistic integrity. On this basis "Ruins of a Great House" sets forth the various levels of reconciliation and compassion (black and white, Old World and New, private and West Indian) as distinct but interrelated aspects of the poet's consciousness *as poet.*

As he develops the poem's fundamental theme of conciliation Walcott pointedly draws upon a set of literary references: he is conscious of being similar to Kipling in that he too is listening to the voice of an empire, though, of course, without Kipling's jingoism; and while he exposes the moral failure of the West he identifies his poetic vision with the voice of one of its moral idealists—John Donne and his "ashen prose." The eventual self-acceptance of the West Indian's diversity is therefore also an emphasis on the process of compassionate reconciliation and complex vision that is inherent in his art as West Indian poet. If the West Indian is a New World Adam creating a new culture out of the rot of the past, the West Indian poet is also an Adam, imbuing places and experiences with significance and identity in the very process of naming or describing them—as he does in "A Sea-Chantey" and "Nearing La Guaira." The vigor and vitality of the poet's personal resolutions merge with the power of the (poetic) Word.

II   The Castaway

In *The Castaway* collection Walcott's emphasis on the artist's role is more overt, and the impressions of the artist's personality as a central and dominant issue are more pervasive. Even more than in the previous collection the themes of this volume are held together by images that have been deliberately filtered through the eye of the poet. The "starved eye" of the castaway figure peers out from the opening line of the collection, in the title poem, and that image offers an early introduction to the theme of perception which dominates the collection as a whole (p. 9). This is the eye of the poet as artist and as West Indian archetype. It surveys the Caribbean in "Tropical Bestiary" and discovers allegories of the West Indian condition, in much the same way that Walcott's postwar contemporaries reject the old Caribbean pastoral in order to perceive the West Indian landscape as a living symbol of the West Indian experience (pp. 19 - 23). But in looking at tropical fauna as symbols the poet's eye is acutely aware, in typical Walcott fashion, of the process by which it transforms the object into symbol. When he describes the man-o'-war bird as a symbol of aspiration in the West Indian's cultural history, the poet's ability to perceive the unlikely bird as a cultural symbol is seen as the microcosm of a larger creative force within that cultural history. On that basis "Tropical Bestiary" has much in common with other West Indian poets who treat the poetic imagination as the symbol of the West Indian's creative national consciousness. But what is noteworthy about Walcott's handling of the standard theme is, once again, that unequivocally autobiographical context, the intense awareness of this kind of poetic vision as something that is taking place within the poet himself rather than being merely an abstract collective symbol. The "I" of the poem is conscious of his creative power as a private talent which has cultural implications for his world and which offers a striking analogy between his private power and the Divine Creator:

> The easy wings
> Depend upon the stress I give such things
> As my importance to its piercing height. . .
> In that blue wild fire somewhere is an Eye
> That weighs this world exactly as it pleases.

On the whole, as this emphasis on the artist's personality increases Walcott exploits it more and more as the symbol of his cultural experience. The intense preoccupation with the artist as both private person and symbol lends itself readily to Walcott's exploration of the familiar archipelago paradox. As an "outsider" the poet is both the archetypal artist-in-exile, the "castaway," and a symbol of West Indians in general as historical castaways from a variety of cultures. And because of this he is in the paradoxical situation of being both the detached, even alienated, observer of his culture and its centrally located, living emblem. In effect the castaway-artist enriches the meanings of that ambiguous island identity which is central to the archipelago theme of Walcott's earlier work and that of his contemporaries. In one sense the circumscribed world of island and individual connotes isolation, even non-communication. But in another sense the isolation of the artist and the castaway history of the West Indian are alike in that both experiences in isolation are a catalyst for self-identification. And in this latter sense it encourages that intense introspection which Walcott derives from the personalized emphasis of his themes, and which results, ultimately, in the redefinition of moral meanings and cultural perception. This explains Walcott's interest, particularly in this volume, in Daniel Defoe's Robinson Crusoe as castaway-exile. In "The Castaway," for example, Crusoe's isolation inspires an introspectiveness that is essentially creative because it contemplates a universal order in which the creation of individual selfhood is at once God-like and analogous to the artistic imagination. In ethnic terms, the white Robinson Crusoe, overlord of the non-white Friday, now represents the self-identification of West Indian castaways from Africa and Asia as well as Europe. He is, simultaneously, an example of the artist, the castaway West Indian, and all alienated, isolated beings.

But he is, preeminently, the solitary individual whose private experience dramatizes all of these moral and cultural meanings. As the symbol of individual imaginations that create in utter isolation he is

analogous to Adam, for as artist and as New World Adam the West
Indian Crusoe defines his identity and environment in the act of
naming them. Hence in "Crusoe's Journal" Adam "speaks that
prose / which, blessing some sea-rock, startles itself / with poetry's
surprise" (p. 51). The emphasis on the isolated individual allows
Walcott to explore yet another aspect of the paradox of the island
identity: the discovery of a crowded, interconnected universe, and
of a closely knit West Indian consciousness, takes place in the
solitude of self-analysis; one senses the infinity of things within the
finite world of the island, and the connections between all things
within the solitude of self. In metaphorical terms, the "eye" of
"The Castaway" sees infinity in the horizon even as the castaway
beholder stands within the symbolic enclosure of beach and sand:

> The starved eye devours the seascape for the morsel
> Of a sail.
> The horizon threads it infinitely. (p. 9)

Moreover, the isolation which has been the catalyst of self-
discovery and knowledge of others has also encouraged the need to
communicate the castaway's perception to his newly discovered u-
niverse. But the very insights which he has derived from a perceptive isolation also separate the castaway-artist from others. Not only
does isolation engender perception, but in turn, perception inten-
sifies one's separateness from others—especially the less perceptive
others. In effect Walcott's relentless insistence on the realities of individual (as opposed to group) experience allows him to avoid
simplistic notions of the artist as seer and leader. And in so doing he
offers sobering insights into the relationship between the creative,
exploring artist, and the cultural group on whose behalf the artist
speaks. There is no easy, transcendental togetherness between artist
and group here, none of that facile identification between artist and
"masses" which has proved the undoing of lesser poets. Precisely
because he insists on examining the cultural significance of art and
artist in specifically individual terms, Walcott easily emphasizes the
fact that, notwithstanding the idealistic criteria of visionary or
revolutionist, the artist may owe his cultural insights to the kind of
introspective isolation which separates him from his social environment as a whole.

In turn, the central ambiguity of Walcott's poetic personality
rests in the fact that his sense of separation is continually counter-

balanced by the impulse to communicate, especially those insights which he shares with other poets—that is, the West Indian's adaptation of the imperial language as cultural tool ("Crusoe's Journal"), the creation of an identity from the nothingness of the Middle Passage history ("Laventville" and "The Almond Trees"), and finally the West Indian's role in salvaging the tarnished New World ideal by making the promise of new beginnings a reality ("Crusoe's Journal"). In the final analysis, however, the underlying motive in these attempts at communication is highly personal. For without negating the significance of communicating with the world around him, the castaway-poet is primarily concerned with communication as an act of self-expression; for self-expression completes and celebrates that process of self-exploration and self-acceptance which characterizes the creative imagination of the castaway individualist. Consequently, the real significance of Walcott's castaway-poet for the West Indian experience does not lie in the role of seer or leader as such (and here Walcott clearly parts company with writers like A. J. Seymour). Instead he is significant as a symbol: he represents the process by which the West Indian as ethnocultural castaway creates and gives expression to a new identity and culture.

III   The Gulf

In the next volume of poetry, *The Gulf*, Walcott's poet is marked by an even greater sense of separation. And this greater isolation is paralleled by the divisions, or gulfs, which the poet himself perceives in the world around him. In fact the poet's personal sense of alienation and separation is really a private extension of the divisions which he sees in the world of the 1960's: the Vietnamese war ("Postcards"), racial violence in the United States ("Blues"), and the civil war in Nigeria ("Negatives"). The gulf is everywhere, compelling our awareness of the very real divisions which mock our most passionate attempts at unity or intimacy: marriage is a "chasm" between twin beds in "Goodnight Ladies, Goodnight Sweet Ladies" (p. 57); in "The Cell" sex is not a union but a coupling that is fierce as that of wasps "exchanging venom" (p. 58), and in "Miramar" it is a grotesquely isolated spectacle—the "mechanical lurch" of a strip-teaser's crotch (p. 20).

The Caribbean landscape itself reflects the human gulf. In "Air" it is an unrelieved void that has devoured everything, leaving only "too much nothing" (pp. 36 - 37). In "The Gulf" it is represented by the Gulf of Mexico, and by the sense of separation that the poet experiences as his jet airliner takes off from Dallas' Love Field. On the whole the poem's impressions of a destructive separation have transformed the United States from the symbol of New World hope and beginnings into a sign of individual alienation ("we leave Love Field"), and the violent betrayal of old ideals in racial conflict ("the divine union / of these detached, divided States, whose slaughter / darkens each summer now"). And the prospects for the future are not reassuring: "The Gulf, your gulf, is daily widening." That grim warning is not limited to the United States. Since America is the poet's symbol of the human condition of the 1960's the phrase, "divided States," extends the American experience of disharmony to all nations and to all states of being. And finally, the phrase, "your gulf," is more than a wry reminder of America's hemispheric possessiveness; it is also addressed directly to Walcott's collective readership, involving us all in the "gulf" of conflict and separation (pp. 27 - 30). In effect the intense alienation which the poet experiences in his own private world and which is reflected in the (New) World around him, has acquired an additional personal dimension by being traced, directly, to the individual personalities of Walcott's readers.

However, the bleakness of Walcott's vision of the gulf is proportionately offset by his faith in the individual capacity to create a fulfilling identity and role from the void of the gulf. In "Metamorphosis" that capacity is analogous to the transforming power of the artistic imagination. Indeed, to be capable of renewal and rebirth is to become a kind of poem: "I am becoming a poem . . . . / My own head rises from its surf of cloud" (p. 12). The individual's personal growth duplicates the creativity of the poet and it represents a larger social process. In "Mass Man" the flamboyant costumes of carnival provide specific individuals with art forms (the folk art forms of calypso and masquerade) through which the drabness of everyday life is transformed into "corruscating mincing fantasies": one man becomes a lion, another assumes the guise of a "gold-wired peacock," and Boysie "barges / like Cleopatra down her river, making style" (p. 19). The carnival figures are therefore akin to the imaginative rhetoric and visions of the poet's art. They are metaphors, highly personal images of the manner in which each individual (a black civil servant or Boysie) or artist (poet, calypsonian, or masquerader) imposes a creative sense of pattern and identity on the drab nothingness of the "gulf." To "make style" by way of music, dance and mask is to create, through folk art, a form of self-expression that is as much a form of self-identification as is the "style" of the poet. Even more than in *The Castaway* the poet's awareness of an analogy between his art and the collective experience of the folk goes hand in hand with his insistence on his essential separateness, as poet, from society as a whole. The gulf image is therefore ambiguous. In the more negative sense it is the symbol of the moral void or wasteland that the poet perceives in the world of the twentieth century; but in another, more creative sense, it represents that dynamic sense of isolation through which the castaway artist comprehends his own significance and perceives a moral order, or cultural continuity, in his environment. Thus although the folk art of "Mass Man" symbolizes a transcending of the gulf as destructive void, it is deliberately distinguished from the poet's own art and personality. As a folk form it represents that collective social experience from which Walcott's poet feels perpetually separated. And in this instance that separateness rests not only in the poet's conviction of his essential difference from the others, but also in the limited perceptions which the poet attributes to the mass celebrations of the carnival masquerade.

The carnival may not only be a form of transcending the void of Caribbean poverty and individual limitations; it may also be a mere form of escape into "mincing fantasies." At best Boysie and his kind are capable of a moving and impressive gesture of affirmation that can only be temporary. After the folk's gesture and celebration conclude with the carnival the void returns for the Boysies of the Caribbean. And even in the moment of that gesture, the poet forces his reader to look behind the masks of the carnival to confront the realities of suffering and emptiness which that grinning carnival mask typically conceals: "somewhere in that whirlwind's radiance / a child, rigged like a bat, collapses, sobbing." Typically, Walcott enforces a sense of his own artistic separation from the world around him at the very moment at which he compels our awareness of the extent to which his personality symbolizes the experience of that world. Consequently, the poet too appears in the carnival masquerade as the hanging whipped body of a slave: "I am dancing, look, from an old gibbet / my bull-whipped body swings, a metronome!" But the nature of the image itself, combining the carnival mask with the Hanging Man of T.S. Eliot's *Wasteland*, emphasizes the literary antecedents which distinguish the poet's role from that of his fellow masqueraders. And in the last analysis it is the poet's art that is more enduring, his vision that is more complex and persistent than the short-lived transcendence of Boysie's folk art. Consequently the hanging-man connotations of *his* mask herald the role of the castaway poet whose separateness arises from his capacity for a perceptive and uncompromising realism:

> Upon your penitential morning,
> some skull must rub its memory with ashes,
> some mind must squat down howling in your dust,
> some hand must crawl and recollect your rubbish,
> someone must write your poems.

At a time when there is continuous pressure from the community and artists themselves to identity the artist wholly with a communal ethos Walcott is strikingly candid about the essential separateness of his role as poet. Yet, as has been noted, this separateness does not involve total alienation. The poet still feels and responds to the concept of a committed art ("someone must write your poems"); but in emphasizing the isolation of his castaway, poetic self, Walcott leaves the impression that those poems may describe, even symbolize the experience of the folk without necessarily presuming that the folk and the poet are one. For it is precisely Walcott's emphasis that they are not one, however much they may be symbolically and analogically related to each other. At a time when the middleclass poet-intellectual is tempted to "legitimize" his or her art by basing it on sentimentally heroic images of the folk, Walcott dramatizes the persistent isolation of his poetic personality by underscoring his separation from the folk. That he is able to emphasize that separation while at the same time demonstrating the complexity and realism of his social vision is a tribute to his remarkable self-confidence and maturity as a poet. There is nothing comforting about this dual role as castaway from and central symbol of his social experience. It is a difficult, often painful role, in which the poet's conviction of his essential separateness goes hand in hand with the need to write "your poems." His poetry is the direct outcome of his own private odyssey for a complete selfhood, but at the same time it is an allegory of an odyssey for renewed purpose and meaning in West Indian, New World, and universal terms.

IV   Another Life

The poetic experience as a private odyssey is clearly implied throughout the themes of personal self-exploration, self-discovery, and self-expression in Walcott's three earlier collections of poetry. In "A Map of the Antilles" this odyssey becomes explicit when Odysseus himself is transplanted to the Caribbean in order to symbolize the quest by the poet, and by individual West Indians, for human connections which can offset the "dividing grief" of island identity in the West Indies and in the world at large (*In a Green Night*, p. 55). But this odyssey motif is most sustained, and most personal in its development, in Walcott's fourth major collection. Indeed, it dominates the theme and structure of *Another Life*. This continuous work reflects an emphasis on movement as a search or quest; and in turn, this questing vision offers possibilities of change, of substitutes for stasis and atrophy in the poet's world. The second chapter, for example, starts out with the moon (Monday as moon day) as the symbol of change—the life-death cycle of birth, christening, marriage and burial. The negative image of the West Indian as a person without history is replaced by the poet's image of his culture as a dynamic movement-in-time, movement-as-change, change-has-history:

> The sheets of Monday
> are fluttering from the yard
> The week sets sail. (p. 11)

"Sheets" and "yard" are ambiguous, referring both to laundry day in the backyard of a modern Caribbean home and to the nautical sights and sounds of a Middle Passage slave-ship. The ambiguity fosters a sense of historical movement from a destructive past to a more creative set of possibilities in the present. In the distinctly Homeric context of *Another Life* as a whole the African's involuntary odyssey of death in the Middle Passage has evolved into the West Indian's passionate quest for life and national identity. Given that context it is appropriate that the poet envisages his islanders ("the stars of my mythology") as Odysseus archetypes, from the Back-to-Africa Garveyite and his African dreams to Auguste, whose skimpy livelihood as a sailor makes him a "lone Odysseus" (pp. 16 - 22).

The poet himself is such a "lone Odysseus," the one whose personality and individual development dominate and give shape to the work as a whole. His role and insights exemplify the West Indian odyssey in its most intense form. It is the artistic vision, or imagination, which enables us to experience the present "movements" away from the gulf of the Middle Passage. While remaining "lone," the poet's odyssey is a microcosm of the West Indian's quest for wholeness and creativity; and in turn, that quest represents what the New World experience can and should be. Hence Walcott's recollection of the fellow-artists of his youth really describes the odyssey of the castaway West Indian, or Caribbean Adam:

> we were the light of the world!
> We were blest with a virginal, unpainted world
> with Adam's task of giving things their names. (p. 152)

Those West Indian artists who subvert this ideal receive rather short shrift in *Another Life*. In an unusually shrill and polemical piece of writing Walcott attacks facile revolutionists ("syntactical apologists of the Third World") and exploitive intellectuals ("academics crouched like rats"). They are "old toms" whose antics really perpetuate the kind of death-like history represented by the Middle Passage: they are slaves in new garb, "green blacks" (pp. 127 -128).

On the other hand, those West Indian artists whose lives and writings seem to fulfill the odyssey ideal become heroic symbols of the poet's own moral mission and self-awareness. Hence the passionate poetry of George Campbell matches the "exhilaration" which the poet recalls in the personality and paintings of Gregorias, the young poet's confidante and fellow-artist. Gregorias' ebullience, in his life and in his art, also transcends the confinement of his poverty and his limited opportunities, in much the same way that the (Jamaican) novelist Roger Mais asserts a defiant vitality in the midst of his Jamaican slums (pp. 64 - 65). As the young poet's alter ego, then, Gregorias the painter links him with other Odysseus archetypes in the recent evolution of a national consciousness in the West Indies. But in an even more immediately personal way, Gregorias' enormous vitality as artist and individualist prods the young poet's own imagination into its own restless quest for personal and cultural resolutions.

In effect, Walcott is affirming a view of art which he borrows (p. 1) from Malraux's *Psychology of Art:* the artist develops within the context of an artistic tradition rather than with sole or exclusive reference to his cultural milieu; more specifically, the maturing poetic imagination is more directly shaped by its interaction with other artists than it is by the raw materials of his environment. The environmental influence is not dismissed, but it is placed on a secondary level. Young Walcott's personal intimacy with Gregorias and his art is therefore chiefly responsible for the poet's immersion in the kind of folk experience which the peasant-painter represented: he learns the affirmative, transcendental function of art like Gregorias' and others like him. And in all of this that personal intimacy reinforces the poet's sense of the individualistic nature of his own art even in the moments at which it represents a group or folk experience. Conversely, that attack on facile revolutionary poetry reflects Walcott's scepticism, even cynicism, about claims of easy and total submergence of the poetic personality into a communal or national sensibility. When he refers to Gregorias and other islanders as the stars of "my" mythology, the pronoun is possessively and intensely personal. This is *his* mythology, his story of growth and development as a poet, his self-portrait of the West Indian artist as a young St. Lucian.

As a child-artist he grows up in an ethnoculturally divided world that leaves its mark on his divided consciousness. His intellectuality incorporates both the imaginative vigor of Gregorias' folk art and the colonial's Western heritage of language and literature. His cultural nationalism flows from two different sources, one represented by the "body's memory" of an African past-in-the-present, and the other symbolized by the middleclass, the city, and by the church-door of the white Christian West (pp. 23 - 28). On the one hand his critical sensibilities are shaped by an appreciation for the European masters and (especially in his view of European painting) by a racially inspired obsession with the painter's image of white womanhood:

> I raved for the split pears of their arses
> their milk-jug bubs,
> the close and, I guessed, golden
> inlay of curls at cunt.

On the other hand, his attraction to Gregorias' work is interwoven with a sensitivity to Gregorias' celebration of black sexuality:

> Gregorias
> bent to his handful of earth,
> his black nudes gleaming sweat,
> in the tiger shade of the fronds. (pp. 60 - 61)

Moreover, the differing sounds of language really each represent the distinct cultural elements of his world. The Christianity of the empire is heard in "Jacobean English" (p. 24); but for the young Walcott there is another Word, the sound of "a life older than geography. . . . / Africa, heart-shaped, / and the lost Arawak hieroglyphs" (p. 54). Finally, the contrast between himself as middleclass boy and Gregorias as peasant extends to the differences between their art. Gregorias' is the art of freedom and creative originality—not because he is of the folk as such, but because, unlike the young poet, his spirit and imagination have not been predetermined wholly by an alien system. He paints "with the linear elation of an eel / one muscle in one thought." On the other hand, the art of the young poet is crab-like in its "sidewise crawling," in its "classic / condition of servitude" (p. 54).

Altogether, the divided self of the young poet represents the gulf between separate worlds, each of which represents "another life" to the other. The poet's growth or personal odyssey, therefore involves the fusion of the divided self into a united consciousness without obliterating the distinctive nature of the experiences that he has inherited from either world. This new integrated consciousness constitutes *another* life, the mature completeness within which the poet accepts the diverse sources of his selfhood. Here in a more complex and intense context Walcott is elaborating upon the compassionate process of self-acceptance which informs the much earlier "Ruins of a Great House." But if "another life" refers to the new consciousness into which the poet grows in his personal development, it also refers to the collective West Indian experience which the poet's maturity symbolizes. In archetypal terms, the poet's emerging consciousness is the symbol of the other (that is, collective, rather than "lone") dimension of the Caribbean odyssey. Once again, without even attempting to posit himself as spokesman *per se* and without negating his insistence on his essential aloneness, Walcott presents his growth as something that is at once uniquely personal and archetypally West Indian—in much the same way that that national West Indian consciousness is both distinctly West Indian and representatively universal. Indeed in Walcott's work West Indian poetry achieves its most succinct, yet complex, statement of a theme that has persisted in the literature ever since Walter Lawrence: the quest for national consciousness and identity is not only a localized cultural act, but it is also a reflection of every individual's need to achieve a sense of complete or creative selfhood; and on this basis the individual or national consciousness of the West Indian is developed in response to a universal need.

Moreover, that child-image through which Walcott develops the quest for identity also has archetypal implications. The image reinforces that sense of new beginnings which is intrinsic to the New World ethos. It also knits together the typical Walcott themes of art as creative change: the image of the child connotes a birth, the wresting of life (a vibrant national consciousness) from death (the long-lived, traditional assumption that the West Indian present, like its past, is mere "nothing.") The positive connotations of "another life" therefore enforce the theme of transformation in both the poet's personal life and in the collective experience of West Indian history. The divided life has undergone the metamorphosis that results in a complete sense of identity. The old "nothings" have become everything:

> that child who puts the shell's howl to his ear,
> hears nothing, hears everything
> that the historian cannot hear, the howls
> of all the races that crossed the water,
> the howls of grandfathers drowned
> in that intricately swivelled Babel,
> hears the fellaheen, the Madrasi, the Mandingo, the Ashanti,
> yes, and hears also the echoing green fissures of Canton,
> and thousands without longing for this other shore
> by the mud tablets of the Indian Provinces. (p. 143)

To hear the destructive nothingness of the past and to accept what is heard as part of a creatively evolutionary process *is* to hear everything: it is to redefine "history" from a narrowly intellectual notion of building (monuments and empires) into the self-redeeming, self-accepting "story" of one's person, culture, and of one's ultimate significance in the universal order of things. Finally, the child-poet archetype represents West Indian poetry itself as a young and growing tradition that draws upon (or listens to) a rich heritage from the Old Worlds of Africa, Asia, and Europe as well as from its distinctive New World experience. The poet has offered his youthful odyssey as an allegory of the directions of West Indian poetry. The gesture not only documents Walcott's enormous self-assurance regarding the significance of his own role as poet; it also marks a new level of confidence in the vitality of West Indian poetry, not simply as a collection of works by diverse individuals, but as a growing tradition with a future. Clearly that confidence in the strength and vitality of West Indian poetry as a tradition also explains the ease with which Walcott asserts the robust, even imperious, quality of his individualism as poet. His is the kind of poetry which assumes that the tradition has come of age and is capable of sustaining the distinctive individualism as well as communal sensibilities of its poets.

CHAPTER 6

The Cyclical Vision
of Edward Brathwaite

I T has become a custom in West Indian criticism to dis-
cuss Walcott and Brathwaite as opposites.[1] Walcott himself
ventured some scepticism about the Walcott-versus-Brathwaite
debate, preferring (as he did during a visit to the University of
Southern California in 1974) to emphasize the similarities between
himself and Brathwaite. The interest in drawing comparisons and
contrasts between the two is inevitable, given the fact that they
have been easily the most dominant and significant West Indian
poets, especially since the 1960's. And by a similar token, Walcott's
impatience with the emphasis on the differences between himself
and Brathwaite is understandable since there has been a tendency
to describe them in exclusive terms—Walcott as the Western-
oriented craftsman and individualist and Brathwaite as the epic
poet and master seer of the black diaspora. In fact there are enough
similarities to justify Walcott's impatience. From a general
historical point of view their works are the culmination of major
developments in modern West Indian poetry—an intensified ethnic
awareness, a growing national consciousness that seeks to accommodate the cultural diversity of the West Indian's cultural sources,
and a complex perception of the destructive energies and creative
aftermath of the past. They also write well within the major directions of contemporary West Indian poetry in that their work reflects
a highly self-conscious preoccupation with the artist's identity and
role in the national culture: they both share with other poets an ambivalent vision of the West Indian's Middle Passage history,
perceiving it as a symbol of dispossession and death but
simultaneously transforming it into the symbol of a continual
odyssey for new beginnings. And in this connection both poets
share historical perspectives and cultural symbols that are in-

terwoven with a New World ethos. Finally the West Indian's moral
and nationalist odyssey in the New World is symbolized by the artist himself.

There are differences too, of course. But these should be considered in relative rather than absolute terms. Brathwaite's trilogy,
Rights of Passage, Masks, and *Islands,* constitutes an epic of sorts on
the black West Indian's history and culture.[2] But neither is Walcott
indifferent to black ethnicity as such: indeed it is integral to his
perception of the West Indian's hybrid cultural personality.
Brathwaite also underscores that duality, in a rather different context. In Walcott's work black ethnicity is tempered by an emphasis
on his personal closeness, by way of his white grandfather, to the
white Western fact. In Brathwaite the West lacks this personal immediacy, but there is a correspondingly intense awareness of the
nuances of being black in the West *and* in Africa. Walcott's Africa is
a mere memory, often vague and beyond physical or psychological
reach. But Brathwaite's Africa is presented as a personal encounter
and as an immediate fact. Walcott's white grandfather and his
English memories (inherited from the ambience of his grandfather's
world) come easily to the surface of his work. Brathwaite has had a
fairly substantial experience of Africa (especially West Africa), having taught in Ghana from 1955 to 1962 after graduation from Cambridge University. Moreover his academic career as historian at the
University of the West Indies and in his island home, Barbados, has
extended his intellectual immersion in Africa and in the black
diaspora. And altogether this personal experience informs the poetic
memories of the continent in his trilogy. On the whole Brathwaite's
work reflects his far greater interest in the cultural transmissions
from West Africa to the New World, and in the organic links
between the West Indian and the West African experience, past and
present. But he can be as sensitive as Walcott to the nuances and
literary significance of the Western dimension in Afro-Caribbean
culture. Hence *Islands* is dominated by echoes of Western poetry
and religion, especially by way of Eliot's *Wasteland,* just as much as
the modes of Akan culture dominate the language and perception of
Masks.

Finally, although both poets clearly address themselves in a
positive way to the ethnocultural experience in the West Indian's
nationalism, their approaches are shaped by their respective interests in group versus individual. Walcott's preoccupation with
isolation as a universal and persistent condition does not allow him
Brathwaite's relatively optimistic assumptions about the realization,

or possible realization, of an ongoing ethnic group experience. In Walcott the reader is ever aware of the primary needs, self-conflicts, and self-acceptance of the individual: the individual stands outside the group experience, especially if he is the artist himself, and at its closest his relationship with the group is symbolical or analogical. The group experience is not unimportant but its primary significance is derived from the extent to which the group symbolizes, contributes to, or is an analogy of, the private experience of the individual. Brathwaite's work reflects a more immediate, less reserved reaction to the burgeoning black ethnicity of the 1960's. His poetry does not dispense with individuals as such, but the greater emphasis is on archetypes who are intrinsically bound up with, and lead the reader directly into the group experience of which they are a part. Both poets are sceptical about the facile rhetoric and built-in delusions of much ethnic politics and many national postures, but Brathwaite is more committed than is Walcott to the exploration of ethnic and national consciousness in terms of their group manifestations. This distinction between both poets is also pertinent to their perception of the poetic role. As already suggested, Walcott's highly individualized themes are an extension of his preoccupation with the poet as private person: his themes evolve from the more archetypal dimensions of the castaway poet in earlier works to the decidedly autobiographical framework of *Another Life*. His poet remains a private individual with public significance rather than the artist who is totally defined by the public function of his art. But in Brathwaite the artistic identity is a composite or collective persona. The "I" of his trilogy seldom, if ever, acquires the private identity of Walcott's poet. In *Masks*, for example, the "I" represents (1) the precolonial African on the historical quest from old kingdom to new worlds in West Africa (2) the African river over which the migrating African must cross, and (3) the West Indian who visits West Africa as an ethnocultural pilgrim of sorts. Brathwaite's "I" is the communal voice speaking out of and demonstrating the cycles of black New World culture in time and space—in the West African past and present, and in the New World past and present.

I   Rights of Passage

Rights of Passage concentrates on blacks in the Americas, moving from the West Indies to the United States and back. The second book, *Masks*, reverses the Middle Passage voyage by returning the reader to Africa. Finally, *Islands* is both a return to the contemporary West Indies and a symbolic retracing of the original voyage of enslavement. The odyssey or journey motif of the trilogy dramatizes the nature and function of the artistic imagination in the black experience: art is a journey through time as well as space; it is an act of memory, discovering and imitating the cycles of history, and in the process both creating and demonstrating a heightened new awareness of the past in the present. Consequently the work song with which *Rights of Passage* opens exemplifies art as an act of memory:

> Drum skin whip
> lash, master sun's
> cutting edge of
> heat. . . . (p. 3)

As West Indian folk art the song re-enacts the black New World history of hardship and pain. The skin of the drum imitates the beaten skin of the slave; but the image of heat not only recalls the suffering of the plantations in the West Indies, it also re-experiences the suffering of those precolonial West Africans searching for new homes on the continent, and subsequently, the disaster overtaking those new homes when they were burnt down by the slavetraders. Conversely, art as memory moves in the opposite direction in time, recollecting the Middle Passage journey which followed the slave-trader's raids. Here it is the gospel song motif that is dominant, emphasizing the Christian forms which Afro-West Indians have incorporated into their culture and which were betrayed by the white Christians in order to establish the slave sources of Afro-West Indian culture:

> How long
> how long
> O Lord
> O devil
> O fire
> O flame
> have we walked
> have we journeyed
> to this place (p. 8)

That reference to movement or journey not only underscores the theme of exile in the history of the black diaspora. It also dramatizes the migratory role of the exile's memory and of the artist's imagination. On a technical level it also complements the manner in which Brathwaite's structure is itself an outward representation of art as movement, as a creative, suggestive fluidity: the poem's form flows from the hard, driving drum rhythms of the work song to the melodious lament of gospel music. The easy movement from one art form to another therefore reflects that imaginative movement or journey which is memory or art itself; and in historical terms, the movement imitates the remembered journeys of the past. But it is also a stream-of-consciousness technique, or more accurately, a stream-of-consciousness experience which is centered on a succession of archetypes. The first of these archetypes is Tom, appropriately so since the popular association of Uncle Tom with an abject servility allows for a typically smooth transition, within the stream-of-consciousness format, from the slavery of the past to a traditional servility. In turn, that transition is underscored by the physical (half-white, half-black) as well as the mental dimensions of Tom's personality. Like the cotton of the slave plantation itself, he is the growth from the seeds of his (white) father's (sexual and economic) needs. But the circumstances of Tom's conception and birth are actually ambiguous. The slave mother's union with the master might have suggested a surrender or an act of apostasy; but it was also fraught with a subversively tenacious commitment to survival and to covert resistance. Appropriately enough, then, the poem's structure shifts to a blues format in the introduction of Tom himself, for the blues is the quintessence of that tenacious commitment. Simultaneously, the total movement from Caribbean work song, to gospel song, to blues corresponds with the gradual expansion of Brathwaite's New World context, from the Caribbean to the Americas as a whole. Conversely, the symbols of black history in the Americas—gospel, blues, the slave plantations, and the Uncle Tom archetype—have been concentrated in the black West Indian consciousness that stands at the center of Brathwaite's themes in *Rights of Passage:* Uncle Tom and the West Indian experience which the archetype represents are linked by their common New World experience.

In more specific terms Tom represents the usual deference and the self-hating acceptance of myths about the racial inferiority of blacks. But considered as a whole Tom is as ambiguous as the circumstances of his conception. His habitual self-negation is actually a thinly disguised mode of defiant survival. The capacity to survive and to create art (music, song, and dance) is integrated with the will

to remember the implications of his racial condition. The Uncle
Tom mask is the *surface* acquiescence of the singer, the clown, and
the carnival calypsonian; but his heart represents a more complex,
less servile response:

> So I who have created
> nothing . . .
> who have forgotten all
> mouth "Massa, yes
> Massa, yes
> Boss, yes
> Baas."
> and hold my hat
> in hand
> to hide
> my heart. (p. 14)

As an archetype Tom's composite language echoes the West Indian
mouthing "Massa," the black American's "Boss," and the black
South African's "Baas." In terms of time the cyclical implications of
the archetype are emphasized by the fact that Tom the rebel-child
of the master must now cope with his own scornfully militant
children:

> "All God's Children":
> They call me Uncle
> Tom and mock me
> these my children
> mock me. (p. 16)

In dealing with the young militants Tom demonstrates the real
complexity of his character by his awareness of the actual
weaknesses of a certain kind of black militancy which, in its own
way, is a kind of Tomishness; for it actually panders to the sub-
human expectations of whites about black violence and black sexuality:

> "Cut the cake—
> walkin', man; bus'
> the crinoline off the white woman,
> man; be the black buttin' ram
> that she makes you
> an' let's get to hell out' a Pharaoh's land!" (p. 20)

Within the memory's cyclical patterns of past and present the ambiguities of an older generation of Uncle Toms have been juxtaposed with the ambiguities of the latter-day militant. The archetypal
mode itself reinforces the cyclical pattern. Hence the Uncle Tom
archetype brings together both past and present in his person, in
that his old-fashioned deference and the bolder "hustles" of the
younger, militant generation are both methods of subversion and
survival in a white world. The geographical cycles (Tom as West Indian, black American and black South African) have therefore been
integrated with the cycles of time and the archetypal mode. Finally,
the poem's exploration of these cycles of being relies on a structure
that is really a cyclical succession of black folk art forms—from work
song, to gospel and spiritual, then on to the shuffle of the sardonic
young militant hustler.

In keeping with the multiple cycles of Brathwaite's structure and
vision Uncle Tom and his militant child are succeeded by the black
"spade" who combines the ambiguities and tensions of both. The
spade's angry sense of identity is compromised by a contemptuous
disregard of history, including his own history:

> just call my blue
> black bloody spade
> a spade and kiss
> my ass. (p. 28)

He is the contemporary urban Black whose self-awareness is punc-
tuated by a sarcastic parody of white perception of the mere
"Negro"; but that self-awareness is diluted by the extent to which
that parody actually reflects some of his real insecurities. The
rhetoric of angry pride masks a basic sense of vulnerability—a striking reversal of the Uncle Tom posture. Hence there is a gradual
shift from the hard, declarative style to the moan of a hurt child ("I
feel / bad mother"). Altogether the diverse rather than one-
dimensional, ways of black folk are demonstrated both by the variety of Brathwaite's archetypes and by the ambiguities and self-
conflicts which he attributes to each archetype. And this diversity is
the direct outcome of the complex awareness and the multiple images of reality which the poet derives from his cyclical approach to
his subject. But the cyclical mode is also complemented by a sense
of evolution or progression that promises some kind of maturing
consciousness. Thus the boogie-woogie beat with which Brathwaite

concludes his description of the spades is laced with the rhythms of a railworker's song: those rhythms reaffirm the continuous, albeit slow, journey towards a robust ethnicity.

The journey motif of the poem is therefore a dual one. It not only describes the cyclical movement of memory and artistic imagination through past and present, but in another, psychologically defined, dimension, it also describes the progression of a certain kind of ethnic psyche groping towards self-definitions that are rooted in humane criteria. This kind of progression has an accumulative effect in that, like the cyclical movement, it brings together the groups and experiences of the New World black—the dreams of Panama boys (West Indian migrant workers at the Panama Canal), the language of the urban black American, and the images of West Indian slums. But unlike the cyclical movement, the progressive structure sets forth these groups and experiences in a sequential pattern. That is, even as one mode (the cyclical) impresses us with the essential repetitions and circularity of the black experience in Africa and the New World, the other mode (a sense of progression) suggests that the archetypes representing those repetitions also establish a clearly defined movement towards a certain kind of perception, as they pass before the reader in succession—Uncle Tom, the black spade, and then the Jamaican Rastafarian (Ras).

This psychic progression is usually underlined in the poem by a corresponding shift in language, a strategy which demonstrates Brathwaite's formidable versality in handling a variety of musical and colloquial rhythms. Consequently the cool, hip bluster of the black spade's American ghetto gives way to the stately flow of Ras' language:

> rise rise
> leh we
> laugh
> dem, stop
> dem an' go
> back back
> to the black
> man lan'
> back back
> to Af-
> rica. (p. 42)

The impressive impact of the language transforms the usually self-deluding Back-to-Africa argument with a new forceful energy: the theme now connotes a racial or cultural rebirth rather than a literal return to Africa, and on this allegorical basis the theme reflects an expanding and aggressive, rather than merely self-defensive or angrily insecure self-consciousness. This moral and emotional incisiveness which distinguishes Ras from the earlier archetypes is heightened by a style which combines the spiritual fervor of the gospel song with the rhythms of the language of Jamaica's urban poor. In one sense the weight of Ras' ethnic awareness and the thrust of his moral outrage do go hand in hand with the pathetic wish fulfillment of an impotent rage—especially when he calls down flames of retribution on an unjust social order:

> from on high dem
> raze an' roar dem
> an' de poor dem
> rise an' rage dem
> in de glory of the Lord. (p. 44)

But in another sense, notwithstanding that element of wish fulfillment, the mere fact of Ras' anger represents a real threat to the future of Babylon (the established order), particularly since Ras' rage, unlike that of the spade's, expresses a fairly coherent and consistent sense of ethnic integrity.

Once again the sense of a progression (represented here by Ras' ethnicity) is linked with the cyclical structure of historical repetition. Thus the threat of a destructive flame in Ras' contemporary Jamaica recalls the fires of death and destruction in the slave-trader's raids of the past. If Ras' consciousness represents a progression of awareness, the flame motif underlines the cyclical persistence of the conditions against which he is striking. Moreover these dual movements of cycle and progression are incorporated in Ras' personality and style. His Back-to-Africa platform repeats a long-lived black dream in the New World, as old as the black presence in the New World; the gospel-song echoes of his language recall the style of Uncle Tom. But, on the other hand, the old Back-to-Africa theme is integrated with the new urgency of a psychological journey of discovery into one's self; and in this vein the contemporary dialect of the urban Jamaican poor expresses the new urgency and a new militancy. Style and structure have become psychological experiences within the poem. This is the kind of dual movement that informs the role of the calypso in the description of West Indian poverty and social injustice. The calypso is a sardonic salute to deep-rooted inequities: *"Some people doin' well / while others are catchin' hell"* (p. 48). On this level its function is cyclical, for it is really a reminder that the injustices of the present, postindependent period actually repeat the harsh brutality through which the modern West Indies were born: "The islands roared into green plantations / ruled by silver sugar cane" (p. 47). But while the calypsonian's song demonstrates the historical cycles of West Indian poverty and injustice, as folk art it is a corrosively satiric insight that represents an attitudinal and strategic progression from Uncle Tom's guileful but self-protective deference.

"The Return" which concludes *Rights of Passage* should therefore be read in the dual context of cycle and progression which Brathwaite has been developing throughout the work and which is so well integrated in the figure of Ras and in the role of the calypso. The physical return of the West Indian migrant from his North American exile represents a full psychic cycle, in terms of memory and in terms of the artistic imagination. For the Caribbean to which he returns is marked by the age-old problems of colonial, or neocolonial, violence (the United States versus Cuba), racial exploitation and anger (Black Power riots in Aruba and Trinidad), national leaders who are under attack for having merely substituted themselves for the old colonial masters, and at the bottom of the pile as usual, the poor who are now beginning to "catch their royal asses" (pp. 61 - 62).

Here too the cyclical experience is integrated with the sense of a progression in the individual's, or more precisely the archetype's, perception. The returning exile therefore communicates a matured consciousness, in contrast with the limited militancy of the spade, for example. That consciousness is manifest in the overview of the Caribbean to which he returns: in other words, the very ability to comprehend the cyclical patterns of West Indian history and culture represents a significant progression from the spade's angry indifference to history. This level of awareness is also implicit in the intensely felt identification with the poor folk, not merely by way of the rhetoric of moral indignation, but also by way of that easy slide into the colloquialism of the folk ("catch their royal asses"): in a work in which shifts in language and style are so closely patterned on subjective experience, that slide into the language of the folk is significant. Moreover this kind of perception is really identical to the perspectives of folk art and Brathwaite's own poetry: it shares with the poetic imagination the creative memory which traces historical cycles, the moral energy to generate a sense of psychic progression, and as a result of all these the ability to see the West Indian situation by being aware of its repetitive inequities as well as its creative energies.

At this point in his maturation our returning exile is ready to re-evaluate Uncle Tom:

> No one
> knows Tom now, no one cares.
> Slave's days are past, for-
> gotten. The faith, the dream denied,
> the things he dared not do, all lost, if unforgiven. (p. 72)

Tom's reappearance heightens the impression of Brathwaite's cyclical structure. The re-evaluation of his character represents the moral and intellectual progression of the exile. That progression is also implied by the more complex view of history itself: the old self-hate and the more recent insecurity of the bellicose spade have given way to a realization that black history can be perceived positively as a creative process rather than as mere "nothing." Creation is the most important kind of historical heritage that there is, especially the kind of creation that is rooted in a growing sense of one's humanity. In this sense history as creation must be distinguished from history as building things through slavery, through the "love- / less toil" of others: it is love, less toil (p. 80). Like Walcott's castaway figure and like the redefiners of West Indian history in modern West Indian poetry, Brathwaite's creators are really analogous to the artistic imagination. And, finally, Walcott's West Indian Adam who bestows new names and identities on the old nothingness of the New World is succeeded in this work by Brathwaite's Noah, that second Adam who stands as a "fully aware" West Indian in the ruins of an old tradition contemplating the possibilities of the new order that must be created, and realizing that there is "no turning back" (p. 86).

II Masks

Masks, the next work in the trilogy, is also rooted in the strategy of developing a full awareness through the cyclical course of memory and art. Here the persistent journey motif describes the West Indian's cultural pilgrimage to West Africa. That pilgrimage is a literal and physical one. But it is also psychic, linking the West

Indian's modern return to his Akan beginnings with the period in
which his ancestors were torn from West Africa by the slave trade
and with that even earlier period when those precolonial ancestors
sought new homes for the first time in West Africa. The total effect
of this simultaneous perception of time cycles is to re-emphasize
time itself as an essentially cyclical, or circular whole. It is therefore
appropriate that the work opens with a ceremony of libation that
celebrates the cycle of time in the year that has "come
round / again" (p. 5). Moreover, this impression of a cyclical
wholeness also rests on the continental dimensions of Africa, the
cultural affinities between its distinctive regions, and most important that cyclical perception of time and experience which the poet
shares with his Africans: "all Africa / is one, is whole" (p. 3).

The making of the drums which follows the libation therefore
becomes not simply the production of an artifact in the Western
sense, but a ritual which confirms simultaneously: the cyclical
wholeness that Akan culture perceives in experience; the manner in
which that sense of wholeness has been transmitted to Afro-West
Indian culture; and a reflection of that wholeness in the actual making of the drum. Consequently, the construction of the drum requires the union of male (the skin of a goat) and female (the hol-
lowed wood of the duru), and this union re-enacts the timeless, universal principle of life and fertility. The combination of the duru
wood with the goatskin rather than with the more traditional
elephant-skin, represents the continuity of West African and Afro-
West Indian cultures since the goatskin drum is characteristic of
Brathwaite's Caribbean. The cultural significance of the drum in
both Akan and Afro-West Indian culture therefore underscores the
poet's sense of continuities—the birth of West Indian culture out of
the enslavement of the West African, the creation of the drum itself
out of the death of goat and tree, and in all these the continuous cycle of life, death, and re-creation. Finally this organic relationship
between the drum and the created world emphasizes that art is not
separate from society and experience but is the very essense of both:
art and artist speak out of and on behalf of a communally perceived
experience in which the drum can be the voice of Odomankoma the
Creator himself.

The drum, itself a symbol of history's cycles, now represents the
artistic imagination of the poet himself in his vision of West African
and West Indian history. The main thrust of that vision in *Masks* is
to bridge the gulf, in the popular imagination, between the West

Indian present and its West African sources, and to demonstrate the
dependence of a vital West Indian identity on an acceptance of the
general wholeness of black history. To these ends the poem evokes
the past and ·the present cycles of West African (Akan) culture in
highly immediate and concrete terms. Consequently the precolonial
West African of *Masks* is never presented solely with reference to
that precolonial history. The drum's recall of the Akan past is the
West Indian's memory of the periods of slavery and colonialism and
the West Indian's impressions of the West African present. The
arrival of the ancestral "path-finders" to new homes in West Africa
is therefore described in terms that evoke memories of the white
slaver's incursion and the modern West Indian's return:

> well have you walked
> have you journeyed
> welcome.
> You who have come
> back a stranger
> after three hundred years. . . .
> So beware
> cried Akyere
> beware
> the clear
> eyes, the near
> ships. . . . (pp. 37, 41)

Whereas the full awareness into which the archetype grows in
Rights depends upon accepting the cycles of New World history, in
Masks that progression is now integrated with an awareness of the
cycles of West African and New World history. To grasp the West
African past in its totality is to come to terms with the complex
nature of the West Indian identity, black history, and the nature of
history itself. The West African market with its flies "clotting" the
entrails of the meat stalls and with its trinkets pulls the memory
back to the slaver's trinkets which led to the blood-clotted birth of
the West Indies. The fallen trees of Nyame the African Creator
have given way to the Christian cross, and the Christian's bells have
silenced the drums of the African God; but in contemplating these
West African endings in the present, the West Indian also
acknowledges a sense of kinship, which signals the new beginnings
of his self-identification:

> My scattered
> clan, young-
> est kinsmen,
> fever's dirge
> in their wounds,
> rested here. (p. 47)

The return of the West Indian is therefore a total immersion into both his past and present, or to borrow Brathwaite's imagery, he has returned "eating time like a mud-fish" (p. 51). And this kind of immersion is emphasized by the poet's language. His contemporary English is endowed with rhythms and with a metaphoric texture that recaptures the cadence of the Ashanti king's ceremonial exchange with his subjects:

> When the worm's knife cuts
> the throat of a tree, what will happen?
> It will die
> When a cancer has eaten the guts
> of a man, what will surely happen?
> He will die. (p. 58).

In invoking the cadences of the Akan language, Brathwaite creates a linguistic symbol of his West Indian's immersion into the West African sources of his identity. In turn that immersion confirms the essential connections between things, beings, and eras in the wholeness of experience, connections that are celebrated here by the precise network of question-and-refrain between king and subjects. And the West Indian's immersion into the African's ceremonial reminder of life-and death is essential to the West Indian's rebirth into a nenewed cultural identity. This too is the function of the mask. In donning the Akan mask the West Indian assumes the spiritual and cultural significance that is inherent in the mask as it is in the drum:

> . . . I return
> walking these burnt-
> out streets, brain limp-
> ing pain, masked
> in this wood, straw
> and thorns, seek-
> ing the dirt of the com-
> pound where my mother

> buried the thin breed-
> ing worm that grew
> from my heart. (p. 65)

In effect, his cultural self-exploration by way of the art of the mask exemplifies the function of art as memory.

III   Islands

The circular movement of art and memory also takes us back, in the other direction, to the Caribbean starting-point of *Rights of Passage*. And this return is the main subject of *Islands*, the final book of the trilogy. The major divisions of this work are centered on the growing consciousness with which the West Indian returns from the memories of, and journey to Africa, "New World" therefore represents both the New World ambience of the West Indian and the new possibilities that are inherent in the West Indian's re-created consciousness; "Limbo" recalls the legendary roots of the dance as an exercise for slaves immediately after disembarkation from the slave-ships, and in so doing it celebrates the West Indian endurance despite slavery; "Rebellion" offers reminders of the old plantation systems, emphasizes their continuation under new, post-colonial disguises, into the present, and by virtue of those reminders its title becomes a prophecy or threat; "Possession" picks up the rebellious, transforming energies of "Rebellion" by offering the contrast between islanders as possessions and islands as symbols of a new dignity or integrity: "possession" as spiritual possession (in the manner of folk religions from Africa and the West) therefore celebrates the new, aggressive consciousness within Brathwaite's West Indian. And in a fitting conclusion to the circular structure of the trilogy as a whole, the carnival dance of "Beginnings" recalls the folk songs and dance with which *Rights of Passage* opens: in this concluding section the dance celebrates the beginnings of a national consciousness that has been derived from the total experience, or historical "rites," of the Middle Passage.

On the whole the return to the West Indies is marked by an awareness of African cultural traditions interacting with a dominant Western culture. The black musician's saxophone recalls Nairobi's male elephants uncurling their "trumpets to heaven." But the setting ("pale rigging") is decidedly Western, presided over by the North American God of "typewriter teeth" and glass skyscrapers (p. 3). But, in turn, that Western God coexists, in the West Indian's

perception, with the African-derived Jah of Jamaica's Rastafarians
and with Ananse, the West Indian folk hero who traces his lineage
back to the spider-god of the Ashanti past. Ananse's webs are the
visual counterpart of the "webs of sound" which are the musical
and linguistic links between the West Indies and West Africa, past
and present; and he is the emblem of the contemporary West Indian spinning webs of memory to fashion a new identity: he is the
artist, existing at the center of the historical and communal patterns
that represent his West Indian experience. Ananse as African
archetype and Afro-West Indian artist is also counterbalanced by
the symbols which Brathwaite adapts from Western literature to his
West Indian themes. In the West Indian beach setting the one-eyed
merchant-sailor of Eliot's *Wasteland* appears in the
"bleached / stare of the one- / ey'd beach." The Caribbean fisherman repairing his nets recalls the life-death eternity of Eliot's Fisher
King; and he is also endowed, by way of his blindness, with the
poet-seer identity of Eliot's Tiresias:

> his eyes stare out like an empty shell,
> its sockets of voices, wind,
> grit, bits of conch, pebble;
> his fingers knit as the dark rejoices. (p. 11)

The life-death cycle that is represented by the Fisher King and the
cosmic perception of the artististic imagination are now being
represented by Western versions of the African symbols through
which Brathwaite has been examining his West Indian situation.
And as an artist knitting the "embroideries" of his net the West Indian fisherman duplicates both Eliot's Fisher King and the figure of
Ananse the Ashanti spider-god. Finally, the Dahomean deity,
Legba, is both the vodun ("voodoo") God of Haiti and, by virtue of
his lameness, the Fisher King archetype of life-and-death in
Western mythology. In short the poet's imagination has transformed the Western wasteland into a fertile source of symbols and
archetypes that duplicate or supplement the African sources of the
West Indian's identity. These Western symbols are being
transformed into modes of an Afro-West Indian consciousness, just
as the chain-shackle emblems of Western slavery have become
sounds of a joyous masquerade of self-affirmation: "Shackles
shackles shackles / are my peace, are my home / are my evening
song"(p. 19).

In musical terms, the Afro-Western synthesis is symbolized by the pocomania drums which recall the drums of the Akan god *(Masks)* who is dumb until the drum speaks, and which express the synthesis of Western and African religions in Afro-West Indian folk worship; and the steelband music of the carnival is another symbol of the synthesis—Afro-Caribbean rhythms pounded out of the oil drum discards of Western technology. In terms of ritual, the rites of the African drum in the Akan past have given way to the rites of cricket, one of the more enduring ceremonies of British rule. But the language and perception suggest that here too the inherited tradition has been transformed into a vital self-expressiveness:

> Boy, dis is *cricket.* . . .
> all de flies that was buzzin' out there
> round de bread carts; could'a hear
> if de empire fart. (p. 45)

On the one hand, the speaker's enthusiasm for cricket amounts to a wry tribute to the thorough effectiveness of the game as an imperial rite which subliminally encourages acceptance of the Empire itself. But on the other hand, the fervent partisanship (*our* West Indian cricketers versus the British *visitors*) takes us back to the central issue of the West Indian as rebellious Caliban, subversively adopting the inherited institutions of the Empire. The declarative "dis is *cricket*" implies an assertive kind of redefinition that wrenches "cricket" from the colonizer's polished "gentility" to a candid partisanship; the candor and the self-assertiveness are reinforced by that reference to buzzing flies, recalling as it does the ancestral memories of the West African market in *Masks;* and that ebullient mockery of empire ("de empire fart") carries with it the threat of a detached, even rebellious, perspective.

That rebelliousness is more fully developed in the cyclical motifs of the "Rebellion" section of *Islands.* The contemporary rumblings in Brathwaite's West Indies continue an established tradition of resistance to equally entrenched patterns of poverty and injustice. In this section the ritual of the wake sets the stage for the recall and celebration of the rebellious tradition. From a historical viewpoint, the slaves' wake for the dead acknowledges the death of freedom, but since the Afro-Caribbean tradition of the wake includes the sending of the spirit back to ancestral Africa then the ceremony is also a ritualistic act of memory, a cherishing of the idea of freedom, and therefore a covert form of resistance. Moreover, the destructive impact of slavery is counterbalanced here by the cultural continuity that is implied by the African memories of the wake. Finally Brathwaite's word-play (wake as death ritual and wake as awakening) reinforces the idea of a renaissance from psychological as well as physical slavery—a progression that has evolved through the cycles of black history. Conversely, those whose rebellion has been superficial rather than substantive have emerged as the new successors to the old colonial overlords:

> it is not enough
> to be pause to be hole
> to be void, to be silent
> to be semicolon, to be semicolony. (p.67)

And by a similar token, an escapist zeal for the folk has nothing to do with a genuinely creative quest for a new life. Someone like Tizzic loves the carnival in this escapist sense, using it to get away from the confinement of poverty. But he is really a mere slave of the carnival's heady escapism. And when carnival is finished he is still a slave to the things which prompted the temporary escape: "After the bambalula bambulai / he was a slave again" (p. 105).

On the whole, then, the progression to a full ethnic consciousness in Brathwaite's work does not depend on the exclusive Westernisms of the "semicolon," the semicolonial mentality. Neither is it to be realized through a facile escape to a romanticized image of the folk and of the African heritage. Instead that full consciousness represents the usual West Indian preoccupation with harmonizing European, New World, and African sources. In effect, the progressive development of a mature cultural identity involves the acceptance of the cyclical wholeness of one's history. To grasp one's history and identity in this way is to be possessed, in a manner of speaking:

> A yellow note of sand dreams in the polyp's eye;
> the coral needs this pain. . . .
> And slowly, slowly
> uncurling embryo
> leaf's courses sucking armour,
> my yellow pain swims into the polyp's eye. (pp.75, 77)

The painful metamorphosis from polyp to coral to island is an allegory of that progression which culminates in the spiritual possession of a full awareness. "Possession" in this sense contrasts with the status of possession—as slave or colonial possession. Viewed in this light the leopard which appears in the "Possession" section is Brathwaite's symbol of a collective West Indian consciousness. Its cage is a reminder of its status as a captive, as a possession. And in geographical terms the West Indian's island-identity offers similar reminders about his relationship with the West:

> Caught therefore in this care-
> ful cage of glint rock,
> water ringing the islands'
> doubt. (p. 87)

But the leopard's very awareness of what its cage means inspires a fierce determination to destroy its captivity: it is possessed by the need to be free. And this transformation from possession as subject to possession as purpose conforms with the central course of progressive growth in Brathwaite's work. The "Beginning" segment of *Islands* therefore marks both the end of the old experience of possession and the beginning of a new phase of awareness. In this context the carnival road march is no longer an escape, as it is for Tizzic and for Boysie, his counterpart in Walcott's "Mass Man." Instead it is the joyous celebration of new beginnings in which hearts, "no longer bound," are now making with their rhythms "some- / thing torn / and new" (pp. 112 - 113). The joyousness with which Brathwaite envisages the sense of beginnings, of progressive growth, provides his work with an artfully devised sense of resolutions. The device is not unconvincing: it flows naturally enough from the accumulative sense of progression or growth which the poet derives from a complex, cyclical vision of the West Indian experience.

The final note of joyousness suggests one of the central paradoxes of Brathwaite's achievement: the remarkable complexities which he discovers in the cyclical arrangement of his universe are never really complemented by equally complex emotional responses to that universe. Precisely because Brathwaite's art emphasizes a communal rather than individualized view of the artist's role, his poetry tends to elicit a limited response to his poetic experience as individual experience. He is always brilliant, and he is never simplistic. The carefully controlled vision and the carefully crafted design complement each other superbly, but the designer remains at a far more impersonal distance from the reader than does any other West Indian poet of major significance. This is not a defect in itself: the trilogy does deserve its reputation as the most important piece of West Indian literature on the relationship between the West Indian's Western and African sources. But it does suggest that Brathwaite still has further to grow as a poet, to allow for the development of an emotional complexity and immediacy that will match his formidable insights as poet-historian, and to permit the sense of contradictions which would, for example, balance the climactic celebration of beginnings with a realistic awareness of old attitudes.

CHAPTER 7

West Indian Poetry Since 1960

I *Protest and Nationalism*

ONE result of the dominance of Walcott and Brathwaite in
contemporary West Indian poetry is the danger that lesser
known but highly significant writers may receive far less critical
attention than they deserve. The truth is that while Walcott and
Brathwaite do represent the major achievements of modern West
Indian poetry any satisfactory overview of the literature cannot be
complete if it stops with their work. Taken together the group of
younger writers who have emerged during the postindependence
period are rather diverse in their interests—notwithstanding the intense, sometimes painful, national self-scrutiny which most of them
share. There are some writers who incline towards Brathwaite's
main preoccupation with group culture and history; others are
closer in temperament to Walcott and the private intensity of his
themes; and still others subordinate their West Indian themes to the
revolutionist's vision of the black experience within the Third
World.

On the whole the political intensity which all groups share is understandable, given the turbulence and challenges of emerging
nationhood in the Caribbean. In one sense the political intensity of
this period is comparable with the energetic nationalism and anticolonial themes of the postwar period; but there are some significant distinctions. The more revolutionary voices of nationhood in
the contemporary period are more likely to identify their West Indian situation as part of a global, neocolonial Third World than did
their predecessors. The passionate racial protest of a Claude McKay
or a George Campbell can still be heard, especially among some of
those poets who have been personally exposed to the racial turbulence of the United States during the 1960's. Lindsay Barrett's
"In My Eye and Heart," for example, echoes the clenched-teeth

rage of his compatriot McKay, even though Barrett lacks McKay's complex capacity for both rage and self-analysis:

> A throat alive upon my blood will do!
> An eye will and when I have plucked the ball
> From the head
> I will explore the gaping socket! (*You Better Believe It*, pp. 442 - 445).

The fundamental optimism which informs Martin Carter's political and social themes, even at their angriest, still appears here among these younger writers. But the expectations of new beginnings in the new order of fresh nationhood are often tempered, especially in the better writers, by a sobering awareness of the extent to which the change of flags, constitutions and political leadership has not necessarily been matched by the meaningful transformation of the national order. Even Brathwaite's vision of an accumulative, psychic progression has room for the rage of Ras at the unchanging order of things; and in some of Brathwaite's younger contemporaries the disappointed expectations of nationhood have actually intensified a disillusionment that ranges from a tough, complex realism to a facile, escapist revolutionism.

Finally, the aspirations and conflicts represented by the civil rights and Black Power movements in the United States have found fertile ground in the Caribbean. The young poet Michael Als founded the Young Power Movement in Trinidad, not long after the island was rocked by Black power riots in the early 1970's. And generally, contemporary poets who take note of the black American experience are far more numerous and more vocal than their counterparts in an earlier generation of writers. The intensity and vociferousness of the contemporary group seem to result not simply from the turbulence in black America as such, but also from the fact that the upheavals in the United States were taking place at a time when the achievement, or near acquisition, of independence made West Indians more receptive than ever before to issues of ethnic and national consciousness. In Jamaica, Edward Baugh's "Colour Scheme," written to commemorate the death of Martin Luther King, is one of the better examples of the current West Indian response to the racial experience of the black American. The work is informed by an ironic intelligence that pinpoints the contrasts between the promise and failure of the American ideal, between possibilities of harmony and the persistence of violent discord; and even more soberingly from a West Indian viewpoint, the poem seems to imply that the destructive violence that explodes out of frustration and disillusionment is not, and will not be a peculiarly North American dilemma. Baugh's dominant symbol is the rainbow. Its "colour scheme" is a symbolical reminder of God's promise of peace and life, and its blended hues are also a visual emblem of harmony. But the rainbow, like its perennial pot of gold, has been "only a deception for the eye." The prevailing realities are represented by the colors of conflict (black versus white): "Skindeep excuses are enough / to make a Memphis of the world." God's promise of life has been obscured by the color of violent death: "one red encroaches on the sky." The original rainbow promise has become a grim apocalypse (the "earnest of the final fire") with global implications ("a Memphis of the world") which extend Baugh's themes, disturbingly, from a precisely American context to a world of racial divisions that includes the poet's Caribbean. [1]

II *Wayne Brown*

Edward Baugh's work reflects an appreciable talent that makes him one of the more noteworthy of the younger poets. But thus far his output has not matched the productivity of the four poets who have emerged to be the most distinguished of his generation—Wayne Brown, Anthony McNeill, Dennis Scott, and Mervyn Morris. Of this group Brown, a Trinidadian, is the one most clearly influenced by Walcott (indeed at times Walcott's influence is embarrassingly obtrusive). [2] The title poem of *On the Coast*, for example, probes the island-identity in those terms of private isolation which recall Walcott's gulf imagery—more so, because the poem, like the collection as a whole, is dedicated to Walcott. "Trafalgar" recalls Walcott's Ruins of a Great House" on the basis of the elegaic sadness and subversive irony which both poems share in their historical perception of empire and slavery. Brown's debt to Walcott is also apparent in "Aquarium" where the multiple sections of his structure (devoted respectively to crab, mackerel, devilfish, and electric eel) are modeled on similar works in which Walcott uses specific animals—as in "Tropical Bestiary"—as symbols. In this regard Brown's work belongs to the relatively modern tradition, in West Indian poetry, of using the flora and fauna as incisively functional symbols rather than as mere pastoral adornment. His electric eel, for example, is a tellingly developed symbol of the failures of the modern technology to which Brown's West Indian is an inevitable, but over eager heir. The eel is the industrial world's serpent, and the technological culture is a Second Fall—particularly for the West Indian's Third World which seems to have no alternative except to succumb to the temptations of the machine culture: "men in midsentences stand and gape / Like machines" (p. 16).

None of this is to suggest that the work of Brown and his generation is significant only insofar as they are comparable with Brathwaite or Walcott. Indeed, Brown's main weakness in this first collection of poetry is his tendency of relying too much on the older poet's techniques and language in order to express his own impressive worldview. But altogether the similarities with, and allusions to the older writers have a positive significance insofar as they demonstrate a relatively new and growing consciousness of West Indian poetry itself as an established, or at the very least, growing tradition. To a considerable degree Brown's relationship with Walcott exemplifies and extends the implications of Walcott's own child-image of West Indian poetry as a young and growing tradition in *Another Life:* a younger generation of poets is now doing what Walcott himself does tentatively with his own predecessors (Campbell and Mais, for example) in *Another Life;* they are perceiving and developing their art within what they feel to be a viable tradition of poetry with its own distinguished contributors, distinctive hallmarks, and modes of perception with which the younger poet may now interact.

In other words, the long-lived consciousness of the need to establish a West Indian tradition of writing poetry is giving way, in Brown and his contemporaries, to an awareness of a living and influential tradition of one's own. This kind of awareness clearly represents a major shift from an earlier tendency to rely exclusively on the interaction between older non-Caribbean traditions (English literature, for example) and the growing West Indian forms. Now the allusive and perceptive modes of West Indian poetry are not only external (interacting with the outsider's literary tradition) but also internal (interacting with the major architects of the West Indian tradition itself)—ranging from the humanistic and disturbing perception of the West Indian landscape to the awareness of the West Indian as castaway archetype, Caliban rebel, or self-defining cultural hybrid. That internal emphasis is the inevitable outcome of the maturing national consciousness in West Indian poetry, one that is humanistic and flexible enough to recognize the worth of the outsider's identity and tradition but which is harsh, as it is in Brown's "Conquistador," towards a slavish, neocolonial dependence upon the mother country. The poet has no patience with those who act as maroons and castaways in the most negative sense of the terms, accepting the myth of their own incapacities and waiting "for the bottle / to bring the Word" (*On the Coast*, p. 9).

The anticolonial temper of Brown's work is actually just one aspect of a complex view of the world which bodes well for his future work. Thus while "Conquistador" perceives the empire of the colonizer as a wasteland, "Red Hills" attacks the social meanness and racial self-hatreds that have persisted into the new, postcolonial world. In a similar vein "Drought" exposes the disappointed expectations and the persistent inequities that have undermined the earlier promises of nationhood. On the whole the poem is a good example of that painful self-evaluation that has characterized the themes of national consciousness in the poetry of the postindependence West Indies. The thrust for a vigorous national consciousness has not been blunted; indeed, it has been given added impetus by the awareness of how limited the status of nationhood can be as an indicator of a really creative national consciousness. This is not all self-recriminatory; for if "Red Hills" underscores the internal failings of the new order, "Drought," like the electric eel image of "Aquarium," recognizes the Third World tragedy which Brown's West Indies share with other new nations: the barest necessities of survival compel an acceptance or imitation of technological and social systems that have often proved inadequate, even self-destructive. This Third World uneasiness with established systems often takes the form of an ideological confrontation between revolutionary values and Western-oriented political systems, But in Brown this uneasiness is less specifically ideological. "Remu," like "Aquarium," attacks the inadequacies of the vaunted technology which everyone, regardless of ideology, assumes to be a panacea for all ills. The oil-polluted beaches of Barbados and Trinidad are never featured in the usual tourist guides, but for Brown they represent a sinister and seemingly irreversible incursion: "the oilslicks of the north / crawled south to die on island shores" (p. 21). As for the tourists themselves, they too represent that sinister invasion, the more sinister because their brassy manners are an alien pollutant that the islanders themselves have actively courted and invited. Brown's "Tourists" is therefore strikingly similar to Walcott's youthful "Travelogue" (published in

25 Poems) in that both works envisage tourism as a mutually dehumanizing process for brassy visitor and compliant islander alike. The process also has a wider significance that touches upon the Third World dilemma of choices. The islander is locked into the tourist trade by the structure of his world just as much as the tourist needs the islander to satisfy a neurotic need to escape into a paradise that exists only in his guiltily unperceptive mind.

On balance, Brown's perception of his contemporary West Indies allows for the possibility of genuinely new beginnings, in the usual tradition of rebirth and re-creation in West Indian poetry. The frozen wasteland of Brown's "Soul on Ice," for example, is imbued with a sense of expectancy, "waiting for words" and for "all those truths the prophets told" (p. 41). But there are no fervent guarantees here; and in this regard Brown's reserve offers a very interesting contrast with the more optimistic, less reserved, revolutionism of a poet like John La Rose whose most significant poetry (*Foundations*) belongs to the same period as Brown's, but who actually hails back as political activist and writer, to an earlier generation of postwar West Indians who had yet to experience the disillusionment of a postindependence period. In the context of Brown's imaginative realism the possibilities of rebirth are very limited in the ice-strangled landscape of "Soul on Ice," the impoverished world of "Drought" and the cultural sterility of the middleclass in "Red Hills." On the one hand the promise of a transforming power, represented by the expected word of the poet and prophet, is real and sincere enough. But, on the other hand, the allusion to Eldridge Cleaver's famous title in "Soul on Ice" implies that too often revolutionism remains nothing more than facile rhetoric and grand gestures. Altogether, Brown's awareness of the promise and failure of the revolutionary imagination reflects a certain reserve, even disillusionment, about the ebullient rhetoric of the 1960's and 1970's, both in the black American's revolt and in the culmination of national movements in the Caribbean. But even in its failures the revolutionary imagination earns a certain respect from Brown, for at the very least it does trigger an awareness of the wasteland conditions to which it reacts. "Wide Sargasso Sea" evinces such a respect since it presents the poet's own fantasy as a kind of rebelliousness: in looking at a painting of a slave plantation he imagines the slaves erupting into rebellion. But even here, the total effect is to distinguish between the imaginative power which the poet's vision shares with that of the revolutionist and the self-deluding rhetoric which is often sloughed off as revolution and change. Consequently the poet is very specific in emphasizing that that vision of rebelling slaves remains nothing more than *his* fantasy, however much it might have been inspired by a very real sense of outrage. In the long run it is this unsparing self-knowledge that distinguishes Brown's poetic sensibilities from the simplistic statements of a popular revolutionary ethic.

III   *Anthony McNeill*

Wayne Brown's tough-minded perception of his own art and its relationship with the dominant intellectual currents of his time is obviously comparable with Walcott's unapologetic sense of privacy. But more immediately it also links Brown with the temperament of Anthony McNeill whose preoccupation with matters of form and content is in response to certain pressures on black artists in America. As he observes in the introduction to *Reel from "The Life-Movie,"* his primary concern with aesthetic matters in the composition of a poem would be regarded as immoral, or Uncle Tomish in black America. McNeill's view of the black American literary scene is obviously simplistic, since he has clearly confused one of its parts with the whole, but the statement does offer important clues to the way in which he perceives his own work. As he continues, the composition of a poem should be the creation of an aesthetic object, "getting it together so inevitably harmonious and *right* that the caught energy stays."[3] Now given the highly polished complexity of McNeill's craftsmanship, these protests may seem at first to be merely gratuitous. But his felt need to respond to the functionalist view of art may have much to do with the general tone and import of his work. His own phrase, "caught energy," is an apt description of his art for it combines a harmonizing sense of aesthetic form with a moral and emotional energy that often resembles a kind of violence. And since *any* connotations of violence are sometimes heard, fearfully or hopefully in some quarters, as straightforward political manifestoes, then McNeill's rather anxious self-explanations are understandable enough—despite the impression that in his anxiety to affirm his aesthetic criteria he does less than justice to the functional effect or moral statements of his thematic "energies."

From a certain point of view it is clear enough that the violence of McNeill's poetry is not one of exhortation but the violence that is inherent in the experience that he describes. While the occasional revelation of violence by someone like Lindsay Barrett may be more numbing, and notwithstanding the eternal cycles of pain in the whips, sun, and flames of Edward Brathwaite's poetry, McNeill's slim volume is the most intense and sustained treatment of violence in recent West Indian poetry. As a Jamaican living and studying in the United States during the 1960's and 1970's McNeill is struck by the violence that seems endemic in American culture. It manifests itself in the callous disregard for human life in "American Leader" and in "Who'll See Me Dive?" and "Suicide's Girlfriend" it turns inwards to become a self-destructive obsession. In "Dostoevskian Hero" violence ("a gun or ruler" applied to the ear) may be physical or psychic, but in either event it is essentially self-destructive (*Reel from "The Life-Movie"* p. 14). At the same time, however, violence may also be creative—not destructive. It may be inherent in the energies of a growing awareness that explodes out of the crippling confinements of a limiting world. In "Flamingo," for example, "Mind swipes at the cosmos / with a cramped fist" (p. 10). The ape in "Rimbaud Jingle" embodies this kind of violence as liberating energy. The animal's cage defines the confinement of a world in which his alleged (black) bestiality really mirrors the subhumanity of those who come to stare at him; and in the final analysis the zoo visitors are the ones who are really imprisoned in a psychic cage of their own making. Thus when the ape recognizes *their* psychic cage his recognition becomes a violently liberating act: "I'll slip from my cage and into / the pure life of lions" (p. 15). But in contrast with the general impressions of destructive violence in society as a whole, this kind of creative, psychic violence is localized, even exceptional. Like Wayne Brown and Derek Walcott, McNeill offers no easy vision of a general transformation. The ape's rebirth is limited to himself; and in due course he will be succeeded by other apes who will perform the usual tricks for the spectators: *that* kind of violently destructive reality will persist.

The ethnic significance of the ape as black symbol is more explicit in "Dermis." Here the sexual act between black man and white woman is fraught with the violent connotations of a rape, rape as his black revenge and rape as her white fantasy-desire for the black stud. But, ironically, the real violence in the encounter is the violent distortion of minds that is brought to the sexual act. In the final analysis the black stud's violence is comparable with the ape's in

"Rimbaud Jingle" because it suggests, however tentatively, the beginning of some liberating awareness. As the victim and the mirror-image of the racist's psychic violence he is a human being with possibilities for growth—a "beast with the ache of a man" (p. 23). For that ache is a yearning of sorts and as such it represents an incipient growth into a full humanity from a brutish victim. The sweet ache of male orgasm at the end of the sex act (and the end of the poem) both recalls the pain of the old crippling violence and suggests the burst of new life: appropriately enough, it is the presentiment of a birth-pang that has implications for ethnic identity in the West Indian as well as black American experience. Moreover this ache of spiritual birth also accounts for the terrible beauty with which McNeill invests the ubiquitous John Crow vulture of West Indian poetry. In "Husks" the vulture's ambiguity reflects the ambiguity of pain and violence as forms of death and symptoms of birth. Even as they fly off at the end of the feast the vultures are "still famished, / in an ache for more servings from death" (p. 12). The ache that cannot be satisfied by an endless supply of flesh must therefore be a spiritual hunger. In one sense, therefore, the John Crow is a figure of death, but in another sense it symbolizes the hunger that cannot be satisfied by the merely physical ("husks of the spirit"), but by the vitalization of the spirit itself. Consequently, even as it flies off from one grisly meal in search of another, the John Crow is transformed from "fallen" angel to a symbol of spiritual longings. As in "Dermis," what begins as a degrading and destructive violence evolves into the possibilities for creative growth.

In McNeill this growth or becoming is ethnosocial in its implications but it is also intensely personal in emphasis. Like Walcott's, McNeill's primary insistence is on the individual's sense of being: that sense of being is a microcosm of its immediate social context and of a violent universe; and the possibilities of a general evolution towards a better universe depend, insofar as they exist at all, on the capacity of each, isolated individual for growth rather than on the magic panacea of a general rebirth or "revolution." Moreover these limited possibilities for a universal rebirth are complemented by the weaknesses as well as strengths of the revolutionary or rebellious consciousness itself. The poet's frank insistence on the ambiguities of that consciousness lies at the root of his impressive poems on the Rastafarians. Ras' dreams of freedom and individual fulfillment represent a passionate sense of dignity that contrasts with the cut-and-dried insensitivity of his Jamaican society as a whole. This passion allows Ras to transcend the squalor of his Jamaican slum. On the other hand, the intransigent facts that are represented by that slum mock his dreams of returning to the African haven symbolized by his god Jah. In "Straight Seeking" Jah

> rears in a hundred tenements.
> Missed by my maps.
> Still compassed by reason,
> my ship sails coolly between
> Africa and heaven. (*Reel*, p. 27)

"Saint Ras" also pits Ras' "city of dreams" against the "straight" world of capital, work, and reason. From that world's rational point of view, Ras' "every stance seemed crooked" (p. 28). Despite its self-deluding nature, Ras' faith endows him with a humanity and an integrity which the world of rational order lacks. But those self-delusions are undeniable. In "Ode to Brother Joe" the evocative reggae rhythms celebrate Brother Joe's triumphant sense of self and ethnicity, but that personal triumph is counterbalanced by the very real powerlessness that is dramatized by his arrest (for smoking marijuana):

> Hail Selassie I
> Jah Rastafari,
> and the room fills with the power
> and beauty of blackness,
> a furnace of optimism. (p. 29)

The poem's structure represents the "caught energy" of Brother Joe's spiritual force while at the same time exposing the powerlessness and the fantasies—the "furnace of optimism"—that characterize his dreams. And the total effect of all this is to emphasize the isolated or private scope of Brother Joe's act of self-identification while suggesting its significance for his society and for all human beings reaching for spiritual growth.

IV *Dennis Scott*

It is apparent that McNeill is working within that entrenched tradition, in West Indian poetry, of presenting the individual's private and ethnic awareness as an integrated aspect of universal ex-

perience. Judging by one of Dennis Scott's early works, "Let Black
Hands," this is also his intention: "Song must swell / from native
throats, but tell of all men's state."[4] The statement is awkward,
even unfortunate, both because of that opprobrious "native" and
because of the telltale distinction, rather than the more familiar
West Indian synthesis, between the idea of ethnic identity and the
state of "all men." Fortunately for Scott's accomplishments as a
poet since that early poem, his work has been closer to the established West Indian tradition than to the clumsy definitions of "Let
Black Hands." Much of his more mature work has been collected in
his recent *Uncle Time*, and in many of these poems he
demonstrates an impressive imaginative power in presenting the
West Indian's history and cultural identity on its own terms,
without the need to justify or demonstrate its universal
significance—except by way of implication. And even at that, the
universal significance is posited as a logical aspect of, rather than a
departure from, the ethnic experience. "Infidelities" is a corrosive
exposé of the racial self-hatreds that are endemic to West Indian
society. "Epitaph" is an imaginatively conceived, tautly executed
portrait of a hanging slave that simultaneously evokes the past of
the West Indian slave plantation, the continuing violence of racial
hatreds in the United States, and the universal tragedy of death and
hate. And in "Homecoming" the general passion for a sense of roots
and belonging is intertwined with a vigorous insistence on the West
Indian's national consciousness: the heart "insists on this arc of
islands / as home" (*Uncle Time*, pp. 6 - 7).

"A Comfort of Crows," published separately, is an impressive example of Scott's ability to develop the sense of local identity as an
intrinsic part of a universal order. Besides being yet another testament to the vulture's fascinating hold on the West Indian imagination the poem is a striking image of the universal life-death cycle
presented in the unmistakably West Indian ambience of the John
Crow itself. The vultures are symbols of the death (drought and
poverty) in the landscape beneath them. But their graceful flight
impresses the poet with their "magnificence," a beauty and a
patterned harmony that contrast with the disordered world beneath
them. And the purposefulness of their flight in the search for
carrion suggests a vitality that transcends the very death that they
both seek and symbolize. They are the essence of life perceived in
the very midst of death:

> The ceremonies of their soaring
> have made a new and difficult solace:
> there is no dead place nor dying so terrible
> but weaves above it surely, breaking
> the fragile air with beauty of its coming,
> a comfort as of crows . . . (*West Indian Poetry*, p. 32)

Clearly the poet has slanted his thematic statements to suggest their universal significance, but there is no escaping the concrete West Indian presence that is summed up by the John Crows themselves precisely because as symbols they have become such a hallmark of West Indian poetry. And in this latter regard, there is an instructive example of the manner in which the poet's sense of a West Indian literary tradition—as noted earlier—has itself become a functional, expressive mode within the poetry.

In the *Uncle Time* collection the achievement of "A Comfort of Crows" is matched by two poems, the title poem of the collection and "Squatter's Rites." In "Uncle Time" the familiar, rather commonplace insights into old age and the passage of time acquire an effective concreteness from the distinct Jamaican context through which time is personified and through the peculiarly Jamaican colloquialisms:

> Uncle Time is a' ol', ol' man.
> All year long, 'im wash 'im foot in de sea,
> long, lazy years, on de wet san',
> an' shake' de coconut tree dem,
> quiet-like, wid 'im sea-win' laughter,
> scrapin' 'way de lan. (p. 32)

Uncle Time is also a folk hero, Ananse the spider-god of Akan culture and the "cunnin' and cool" mastermind in West Indian folk tales. And that archetypal reference to the idea of a deity (the spider-god) provides the poet with a distinctly *Afro-Western* image of a *universal* godhead that dispenses life and death to all through time: "Watch 'ow 'im spin' web roun' you' 'house, an' creep' / inside; an' when 'im touch y'u, weep!" (p. 32).

Scott's careful attention to technical details (in this case, language and symbolism) is the key to his successful blend of his Jamaican and West Indian experience with his perception of universal time. By a similar token "Squatter's Rites" explores the usual life-death cycle through the immediate Jamaican presence of old Ras. As the squatter "king" of his "drowsy hill," Ras is the familiar Rastafarian symbol of personal strength in the fragile circumstances of poverty and institutionalized indifference. The death that is inherent in his social condition is confirmed by his eventual demise. But in turn death gives way to rebirth when Ras' son, a reggae musician, buries Ras "with respect" and plays a musical salute to the indomitable and immortal strength of the old man's spirit:

> . . . at night, when the band played
> *soul*, the trumpet
> pulse beat
> down the hill
> to the last post,
> abandoned,
> leaning in its hole
> like a sceptre
> among the peas, corn, potatoes. (pp. 42 - 43)

The "pulse beat" of reggae, the urban folk music, now celebrates Old Ras' personal vitality. In the process his perception of his own dignity has been vindicated by the folk art, and further, by the poet's integration of his own forms with the structure of the folk art. The theme of life-from-death has been extended to the way in which the poet's own art grows out of and thrives upon the sufferings and decay of Ras and his kind. This kind of thematic extension obviously involves a frank recognition, on the poet's part, of the relationship between his own role and the social tragedies that his poetry describes: the experience of Ras and the disadvantaged folk is not sentimentalized, but neither does the poet offer the familiar conscience-salving illusion that *his* art represents an immediate corrective to those disadvantages. Indeed the real contributions seem to have flowed in the opposite direction: Ras' lot and that of the folk have given birth to distinctive styles and forms that now sustain the art and vision of the poet. Finally, however, the poet's relationship with the folk and their art is not merely parasitic; for if the poet has no illusions about the corrective power of his art in the material experiences of the poor and disadvantaged, his vision and even more importantly, his indebtedness to the styles and forms of the folk constitute a tribute to their collective vitality and, individually, to their personal resiliency.

V   *Mervyn Morris*

In effect Dennis Scott has allowed his technical form as a whole
to represent a complex synthesis of the universal (the life-and-death
cycle), the regional (the ethnic and artistic self-expressiveness of the
folk), and the private (Old Ras' personal integrity, for example),
with each element complementing and illuminating the other.
Scott's Jamaican compatriot, Mervyn Morris, cultivates this kind of
complexity in his own perception of his poetry.[5] *The Pond*, his
collection of selected poems, obviously results from a carefully considered choice of works which reflect a variety of themes ranging
from the poet's role in the ethnocultural experience, to the integrity
of the private self. The total effect of Morris' poetry considered as a
whole is the conviction that the general complexity of things
precludes straightforward or unequivocally partisan declarations.
Poetry itself is a highly ambiguous undertaking for Morris, self-
sufficient as art, requiring no justification beyond its own form. But
at the same time it must deal with pressures from within and around
the poet to take a stand, to carry a social banner; and in attempting
to deal with such pressures the poem must, perforce, subsist on a
basis that includes but goes beyond a purely aesthetic self-
sufficiency. The absence of any final sociopolitical commitment in
Morris' work therefore represents a committed statement of sorts:
the refusal to bind himself to any one political viewpoint reflects a
firm commitment to assumptions about the complexity of art and
experience. Poetry is both art and moral statement considered not as
separate and distinct entities but as integrated parts of a whole;
hence to see it merely as aesthetic object, as some would have the
poet do, or only as committed statement, as others would, is to dis-
tort its complex nature. Morris does not reject the value of political
and social statement as such, but he feels that to define the thematic
texture of poetry on the basis of political commitment is to over-
simplify the multiple insights and possibilities of poetry itself.

"Stripper" is one of Morris' more precise acts of self-scrutiny as
poet. As he describes the stripteaser's performance-as-art, the poem
itself progressively becomes the emotional and intellectual stripping
of the poet. The total effect of that stripping is to enforce an acceptance of the poet's art in its totality as both art and performance,
as aesthetic display and moral statement, in much the same way
that the reader is persuaded to accept the stripteaser's performance
as art in its own right. His sexual reaction to the stripteaser

therefore compels our recognition of the parallels between their roles as artists; and in the process it represents the reconciliation, within the poet himself, between art as aesthetic display and art as the complex reflection of a complex world: "She took the last piece off the law allowed / The poet felt his symbol growing hard" (*The Pond*, p. 11).

The poet is also a stripper, not only because of the telling analogy between his art and that of the stripteaser's, but also by virtue of the intense introspectiveness through which Morris actually peels away layers of the poet's consciousness in order to pose questions about the relationship between the poet and his craft. This is the introspective questioning that informs a work like "Satirist" and links the self-scrutiny of the poet with the individual's probing into his private self. In fact the decidedly individualistic rather than group orientation of Morris' art needs to be viewed in the light of his continuous preoccupation with the private worlds within the individual's private self. The inward turning of the artist's eyes is therefore part of the general introspectiveness which also occurs in "journey into the Interior" where "Stumbling down his own esophagus / he thought he'd check his vitals out" (p. 40). In "The Forest" the reader is invited to leave the "certain" world of the sun where nothing is really seen, to experience an interior vision deep in the mind (p. 39). The experience of that inner world is ambiguous. "Journey into the Interior" ends on a one-way note: the way back to the outside is blocked, "so now / he spends the long day groping there, inside" (p. 40). But the act of groping connotes a vigor and an animating curiosity which makes the mind, even the maggotty mind of "The Forest," vital and therefore superior to the limited certitudes of the sunlit world outside.

In "Narcissus" the encounter with the reflected image, that other self, is fraught with the traditionally negative implications. But if self-contemplation is a potentially self-destructive narcissism it leads, above everything else, to an awesome knowledge of self that can actually bring about a profound humility:

> At last he knew
> he never would
> destroy that other self.
> And knowing made him shrink. (p. 43)

"The Pond" is an updated Jamaican setting of the Narcissus legend, and here too the poet emphasizes self-contemplation as knowledge of self. The small boy who braves horror-stories about the village pond discovers himself (rather than monsters and nameless horrors) in its depths:

> Sudden, escaping cloud the sun
> came bright; and, shimmering in guilt,
> he saw his own face peering from the pool. (p. 42)

The need for self-examination, the need to stumble down his own esophagus, explains the poet's desire to be alone. The desire is strong enough to encourage an impatience with family ties in "Family Picture." The external roles of father, husband, head of the household are, presumably, those limited sunlit certitudes which also include political partisanship and ethnic debate. Consequently the zest with which the poet embarks upon his interior visions is counterbalanced by a decided lukewarmness towards black militancy in "Case-History, Jamaica." That lukewarmness seems to result less from scepticism about ethnic pride as such and more from an uneasiness with the shallow vision and facile rhetoric that are often offered as modes of ethnic identity. Shallowness and instability of this kind are doubly unacceptable because they are also such an antithesis to the sure and complex nature of the poet's own self-knowledge. That instability is the more suspect because it seems so repetitive: the "angry promises" of the present generation of revolutionaries are simply reminders of similar promises ("The Early Rebels") by an earlier generation of rebels who are now the complacent "fathers of our nation" (p. 21). Altogether Morris reacts to the political turbulence of his postindependence world with an ironic detachment from all sides. But his withdrawal has the effect of a studied comment rather than mere escape. "To the Unknown Combatant" seizes upon the narrowness and limited humanity of both sides as a basis for refusing to join the right or the left. Even in "The House-Slave" the anger of the modern ex-slaves (ex-colonials) against the house-slave (neocolonial) is as suspect as the house-slave mentality itself; for if the house-slave's servile loyalties and "tutored terror" are contemptible, the other side indulges in an undiscriminating destructiveness now that the "pallid masters" have fled (p. 17). And in "To an Expatriate Friend" there is an evenhanded contempt for both the "loud" anger of a new black intolerance and the familiar narrowness of the white expatriate (p. 14).

This sceptical withdrawal from sociopolitical activism, combined with his introspectiveness, has had the effect of marking Morris as the most private, the least activist in orientation of the major contemporary poets. His suspicious reserve towards radical group rhetoric and politics is not unlike Walcott's scepticism in *Another Life*. But while Walcott effects and maintains a fine balance between a perceptive isolation and the castaway's yearning, albeit a futile one, for a world that he actually symbolizes, Morris actively shuns the possibilities of that kind of contact in favor of a less ambiguous commitment to the needs of the private, interior self. Conversely, his interest in that private self is comparable with the introspective body-consciousness observed in A. J. Seymour's more recent poetry, but Morris shuns that missionary activism which complements Seymour's interest in the poet's private world. It is therefore characteristic of Morris' imaginative bent that the screaming and, more suggestively, the "riot of colour" in "Nursery" are far less interesting than the hidden thoughts of the autistic child in the same poem (p. 12). The implied ethnopolitical statements of "Nursery" are more explicit in "I Am the Man" and "Rasta Reggae," and so are Morris' most fundamental instincts as a poet. The slum poverty of "I Am the Man" (p. 15) excites the poet's sympathy; and there is a corresponding scorn for an insensitive and morally bankrupt officialdom that bulldozes the slum dweller's home, then dismisses him as "the man of no fixed address." On this basis Morris clearly demonstrates that his refusal to be an activist-poet does not preclude his moral and social commitment as an artist. But "the Man" also engages Morris' empathetic understanding because the former demonstrates a powerful self-knowledge which arises out of his condition but transcends it. The refrain of the poem, "I am the man. . ." is the self-affirmation that results from an intense and deep self-awareness. Similarly the familiar Back-to-Ethiopia vision of the Rastafarian, in "Rasta Reggae," is transformed into a profoundly interior vision:

> Release I brother let me go
> let my people go
> home to Ethiopia
> in the mind. (p. 18)

Without denying Ras' cry for ethnic fulfillment and social emancipation, Morris celebrates in the Rastafarian archetype that experience which the poet perceives as the most fundamental and
liberating of all—the full exploration of each individual's private
consciousness both as it reflects and exists apart from the world outside.

VI Conclusion

Altogether Morris' intense sense of privacy as poet places him in
the opposite direction from someone like Brathwaite who insists on
the public role and corporate, communal identity of art as collective
memory. He is as distinct from Brathwaite as the latter is from the
romantic revolutionism which often mars popular notions of the
ethnicity that Brathwaite describes with such compelling insights.
In turn, both Morris and Brathwaite need to be distinguished from
writers like Walcott, Brown, and Scott who consistently seek to en-
vision the private needs of individual selfhood within the distinctive
dimensions of a West Indian, New World consciousness and within
the sense of a shared universality.

It seems fitting at this point that Morris should be the pivotal
figure in an assessment of the present directions of contemporary
West Indian poetry. His relationship with his contemporaries
demonstrates the extent to which that poetry is an essentially
diverse collection of writings that can accommodate the creative
eccentricity of an individualistic author like Morris; and in a sense,
that diversity recalls the total West Indian diversity which Morris
himself once cited, in "To A West Indian Definer," as the basis for
challenging past and precise definitions of West Indian society and
literature.[6] But on the whole the differences within this generation
of West Indian poets are similar to the experience of previous
generations in that they are not fundamental enough to obscure the
common preoccupation with the quality, the directions, and the
definitions of West Indian society and with the poet's role (private,
semi-private, and / or public) in the evolution of a West Indian
national consciousness. And quite apart from this organic link the
divergent approaches and emphases often come equipped with
their own irrefutable truths, truths which all come together to
reflect the multifaceted reality that is the West Indian experience.
Consequently Edward Brathwaite offers convincing insights into
the spiritual richness and ethnic vitality of the folk. And on the

other side Morris' cautious reserve towards group activism, or Dennis Scott's candor about the poet's *dependence* on the disadvantages of the folk, also touch upon another set of truths—such as the one that I experienced in the summer of 1975 when a bus-passenger in Kingston, Jamaica, reacted to a television program in which a local political leader extolled the strengths and productivity of Jamaicans by citing the national achievement in producing reggae music: how, the bus-passenger fumed, would reggae music help her find a badly needed job or put food in her children's mouths?

However possible it might be to establish the common grounds between the main trends in contemporary West Indian poetry, it is still difficult to determine future directions, for taken together or separately these trends are really the formative beginnings in what is still a young tradition of poetry. It is clear, nonetheless, that the contemporary emphasis on the nature of a West Indian consciousness really extends the prevailing interests of West Indian poetry since the turn of the century, but more particularly, since the Second World War. This emphasis lies at the heart of the most vital and challenging works over that period and its dominance in our own time seems to assure that it will shape the course of West Indian poetry in the immediate future—particularly since some of the established writers (such as Mervyn Morris and the Creative Arts Centre of the University of the West Indies, Jamaica) have undertaken to encourage promising new talent. Given the notorious apathy of West Indian readers to West Indian literature, especially poetry, this kind of encouragement is crucial for the emerging writers, although it is not often as readily forthcoming from some established writers as some have hoped.

The temper of the poetry and its sociopolitical environment seems to preclude the kind of mass exile which took the writers of the 1940's, 1950's, and early 1960's to England and elsewhere in search of economic self-sufficiency, but there is little doubt that the limited opportunities at home will continue to push some into exile. But as the number of those who elect to remain at home increases, there will be growing pressure for the institutional and individual support which the University of the West Indies offers through its Creative Art Centre and through poets like Morris who work at the university as teachers and are interested enough to help. This is the kind of help that seems less evenly distributed than it should: it is badly needed in Barbados, Trinidad, and the less populous islands.

As West Indian poetry becomes even more self-consciously, and

insistently West Indian in its immediate motives it must deal increasingly with an old problem which becomes more and more
acute and which plagues highly talented and promising writers like
the young members of the Barbados Writers' Workshop: they need
an audience, now almost nonexistent, that is not exclusively defined
by the interests of the outside anthologist or the foreign publisher,
however much these may be economically necessary and helpful,
and however much outside readers may respond with enthusiasm to
the cosmopolitan context in which the West Indian poet locates his
national consciousness. The most pressing problem for West Indian
poetry at this time, then, is not one of talent. In the truest tradition
of much of the Third World, the resources are abundant enough,
but the means of fair and fulfilling development are inadequate.
And in this regard the future of the West Indian's poetry and of the
national consciousness which it voices are bound up with the
endemic Third World problem of attempting to develop national
resources in a context of international dependency.

Notes and References

Preface

1. Robert Hamner, *V. S. Naipaul* (New York: Twayne, 1973), preface.

2. Cameron King and Louis James, "In Solitude for Company: The Poetry of Derek Walcott," in *The Islands in Between: Essays on West Indian Literature*, ed. Louis James (London: Oxford, 1968), pp. 86 - 99. Cited hereafter as *The Islands in Between*.

3. Edward Brathwaite, "Caribbean Critics," *New World Quarterly*, 5, 1 - 2 (1969), 5 - 12.

4. Sylvia Wynter, "Reflections on West Indian Writing and Criticism," *Jamaica Journal*, 2, No. 4 (December, 1968), 23 - 32.

5. George Lamming, *The Pleasures of Exile* (London: Michael Joseph, 1960), pp. 37, 214. Cited hereafter in the text as *The Pleasures of Exile*.

6. V. S. Naipaul, *The Middle Passage: The Caribbean Revisited.* (New York: Macmillan, 1963), p. 29.

7. Frantz Fanon, *Black Skins White Masks* (New York: Grove, 1967), pp. 17 - 18.

Chapter One

1. James Grainger, *Sugar Cane* (London: Whittingham, 1764). Cited here from *The Works of the English Poets from Chaucer to Cowper*, ed. Alexander Chalmers (London: Whittingham, 1810), XIV, 478 - 511. Noted by James Boswell, *Life of Johnson*, ed. G. B. Hill, rev. ed. L. F. Powell (Oxford: Clarendon Press, 1934 - 1950), II, pp. 453 - 55.

2. Francis Williams, "Ode to George Haldane," in Edward Long, *History of Jamaica* (London: Lowndes, 1774), II, pp. 478 - 81.

3. Norman E. Cameron, ed. *Guianese Poetry: 1831 - 1931* (Georgetown, Guyana: Argosy, 1931). Cited hereafter as *Guianese Poetry*.

4. Walter M. Lawrence, "Guiana," in *The Poet of Guiana* (Georgetown, Guyana: Daily Chronicle, 1948), p. 22.

5. *Orange Valley and other Poems* (Kingston, Jamaica: Pioneer Press, 1951), pp. 8 - 9. Cited in the text hereafter as *Orange Valley*.

6. Agnes Maxwell-Hall, "Jamaican Market," in *3000 Years of Black Poetry*, eds. Alan Lomax and Raoul Abdul (New York: Dodd Mead, 1970), p. 117.

7. Quotations from Una Marson's poetry are based on *Heights and Depths* (Kingston: Gleaner, 1931) and *The Moth and the Star* (Kingston, Jamaica: 1937).

Chapter Two

1. Max Eastman, "Biographical Note," in *Selected Poems of Claude McKay*, introd. John Dewey (New York: Bookman Associates, 1953), pp. 110 - 112. (Cited hereafter in the text as *Selected Poems*); Addison Gayle, Jr. *Claude McKay: A Black Poet at War*, (Detroit: Broadside, 1972).

2. References to these works are based on *Songs of Jamaica* (Kingston: Gardner, 1912) and *Constab Ballads* (London: Watts, 1912).

3. Claude McKay, "Author's Word," in *Harlem Shadows* (New York: Harcourt, Brace, 1922), pp. xix - xxi. Cited hereafter in the text as *Harlem Shadows*.

Chapter Three

1. Wordsworth McAndrew, *Blue Gaulding* (Georgetown, Guyana: Master Printery, 1958), p. 1.

2. Harold Telemaque, *Burnt Bush* (Port-of-Spain, Trinidad, 1947), pp. 7 - 8.

3. Eric Roach, "March Trades," in *Caribbean Voices*, ed. John Figueroa (London: Evans, 1966 - 1970), II, 155 - 56. Cited hereafter in the text as *Caribbean Voices*.

4. Raymond Barrow, "There Is a Mystic Splendour," in *Caribbean Verse: An Anthology*, ed, O.R. Dathorne (London: Heinemann, 1967), p. 16.

5. Carl Rattray, "And Crows Go Circling Round," in *Firstlings: A Collection of Poems*, (Kingston, Jamaica, 1950), n.p. Compare Barnabas Ramon-Fortune, "The Crow," in Caribbean Voices, I, pp. 90 - 91.

6. Roy McFarlane, "Crow Perch," in his *Hunting the Bright Stream* (Kingston, Jamaica: City Printery, 1960), p. 19.

7. Wordsworth McAndrew, "Legend of the Carrion Crow," in *Breaklight: The Poetry of the Caribbean*, ed, Andrew Salkey (New York: Doubleday, 1973), pp. 80 - 81. Cited hereafter in the text as *Breaklight*.

8. William S. Arthur, *No Idle Winds: A Book of Poems* (Bridgetown, Barbados: Advocate, 1954), p. 28.

9. Eric Roach, "I Am the Archipelago," in *You Better Believe It: Black Verse in English*, ed. Paul Breman (Harmondsworth, England: Penguin, 1973), pp. 156 - 58. Cited hereafter as *You Better Believe It*.

10. Andrew Salkey, *Jamaica* (London: Hutchinson, 1973), p. 106.

11. A. L. Hendriks, "To You in St. Lucia and You in Mars," in his *On This Mountain* (London: Deutsch, 1965), p. 35. Cited hereafter as *On This Mountain*.

12. Harold Telemaque, "One People," in *Scarlet* (Georgetown, Guyana: Master Printery, 1953), p. 8.

13. Jan Carew, "Atta," in *Streets of Eternity* (Georgetown, Guyana, 1952), n.p.

14. Frank Dalzell, "Guiana's Voice," in *Moments of Leisure* (Georgetown, Guyana: Master Printery, 1952), p. 7.

15. Ellsworth McG. Keane, *l'Oubli* (Bridgetown, Barbados: Advocate, 1950), pp. 17, 27 - 30.

16. References to Arthur Seymour's poetry are based on his *The Guiana Book* (Demerara, Guyana: Argosy, 1948); *Selected Poems* (Georgetown, 1965); *Black Song* (Georgetown, Guyana: Labour Advocate, 1971); *Italic* (Georgetown, Guyana: Labour Advocate, 1976).

17. George Campbell, *First Poems* (Kingston, Jamaica: City Printery, 1945). Cited hereafter in the text as *First Poems*.

18. Frank Collymore, *Collected Poems.* (Bridgetown, Barbados: Advocate, 1959). Cited hereafter in the text.

19. Martin Carter, *Poems of Resistance from British Guiana* (London; Lawrence, Wishart, 1954). Cited hereafter in the text as *Poems of Resistance*.

20. Wilson Harris, *Eternity to Season* (Georgetown, Guyana: Author 1954). Revised edition published with J. Antonio Jarvis, *Bamboula Dance* (Nendeln, Liechtenstein: Kraus Reprint, 1970). Cited hereafter in the text.

21. Quotations from Phillip Sherlock's poetry are based on his *Ten Poems* (Georgetown, Guyana: Master Printery, 1953).

Chapter Four

1. Walter Jekyll, ed. *Jamaican Song and Story* (New York: Dover, 1966).

2. Olive Lewin, "Folk Music Research in Jamaica," in *Black Communication: Dimensions of Research and Instruction* (New York: Speech Communication Association, 1973), pp. 121 - 35.

3. Edward Brathwaite, *Folk Culture of the Slaves in Jamaica* (London: New Beacon Books, 1970), p. 17.

4. References to Sparrow's songs are based on "Lulu," and "Monica" in the phonograph albums *Sparrow* (Radio Corporation of America LPB - 9035), and "Congo Man" in *Sparrow: Congo Man* (Hillary SP 30006).

5. References to Louise Bennett's poetry are based on *Jamaica Labrish* (Kingston, Jamaica: Sangster, 1966).

6. Reference to the sinking of the German battleship Graff Spe during Second World War.

Chapter Five

1. Frank Collymore, "An Introduction to the Poetry of Derek Walcott," *Bim*, 3, No. 10 (1949), 125 - 32.

2. References to Derek Walcott's poetry are based on his *In a Green Night* (London: Cape, 1969); *The Castaway* (London: Cape, 1969); *The Gulf* (London: Cape, 1969); and *Another Life* (London: Cape, 1973).

Chapter Six

1. See, for example, Patricia Ismond, "Walcott versus Brathwaite," *Caribbean Quarterly*, 17, 3 - 4 (Sept.-Dec. 1971), 54 - 71.

2. References to Edward Brathwaite's poetry are based on his *Rights of Passage* (London: Oxford, 1967); *Masks* (London: Oxford, 1968); and *Islands* (London: Oxford, 1969).

Chapter Seven

1. *Seven Jamaican Poets*, ed. Mervyn Morris (Kingston, Jamaica: Bolivar Press, 1971), p. 23.

2. Quotations from the poetry of Wayne Brown are based on Wayne Brown, *On the Coast* (London: Deutsch, 1972).

3. *Reel from "The Life Movie"* (Kingston, Jamaica: Savacou, 1975), pp. 1 - 5. Cited hereafter in the text.

4. *Focus*, 4 (1960), 29. Other quotations from Scott's work are based on Dennis Scott *Uncle Time* (Pittsburgh: University of Pittsburgh, 1973) and *West Indian Poetry*, eds. Kenneth Ramchand and Cecil Gray (Port-of-Spain, Trinidad: Longman, 1971).

5. Quotations from Morris' poetry are based on Mervyn Morris *The Pond* (London: New Beacon Books, 1973).

6. *Caribbean Literature*, ed. Gabriel Coulthard (London: University of London, 1966), p. 86.

Selected Bibliography

PRIMARY SOURCES

Anthologies:

You Better Believe it: Black Verse in English. Paul Breman. ed. Harmondsworth, England: Penguin, 1973.

Guianese Poetry: 1831 - 1931. Norman E. Cameron, ed. Georgetown, Guyana: Argosy, 1931.

Caribbean Verse: An Anthology. O. Ronald Dathorne, ed. London: Heinemann, 1967.

Caribbean Voices. John Figueroa, ed. 2 vols. London: Evans Brothers, 1966 - 1970.

Independence Anthology of Jamaican Literature. A. L. Hendriks, ed. Kingston, Jamaica: United Printers, 1962.

Jamaican Song and Story. Walter Jekyll, ed. New York: Dover, 1966.

Voices from Summerland: An Anthology of Jamaican Poetry. John E. Clare McFarlane, ed., London: Fowler Wright, 1929.

3000 Years of Black Poetry. Alan Lomax and Raoul Abdul, eds., New York: Dodd Mead, 1970.

Seven Jamaican Poets. Mervyn Morris, ed. Kingston, Jamaica: Bolivar Press, 1971.

West Indian Poetry. Kenneth Ramchand and Cecil Gray, eds., Port-of-Spain: Longman, 1971.

Breaklight: The Poetry of the Caribbean. Andrew Salkey, ed. New York: Doubleday, 1973.

An Anthology of Guianese Poetry. Arthur J. Seymour, ed. Georgetown, Guyana: *Kyk-over-al,* 1954.

New Writing in the Caribbean. Arthur J. Seymour, ed. Georgetown, Guyana: Lithographic, 1972.

ARTHUR, WILLIAM S. (n.d.) Barbados. *No Idle Winds: A Book of Poems.* Bridgetown, Barbados: Advocate, 1954.

BENNETT, LOUISE. *Dialect Verses.* Kingston, Jamaica: Herald, 1942.

————. *Jamaican Dialect Poems.* Kingston, Jamaica: Gleaner, 1948.

————. *Jamaica Labrish.* Kingston, Jamaica: Sangster's Book Stores, 1966. Poet born 1919, still living.

BLACKMAN, PETER. N.D. *My Song Is for All Men.* London: Lawrence, Wishart, 1952.

BRATHWAITE EDWARD. *Masks.* London: Oxford University Press, 1968.

————. *Islands.* London: Oxford University Press, 1969.

———. *The Arrivants: A New World Trilogy*. London: Oxford University Press, 1973. Barbados author born 1930, still living.

BROWN, WAYNE. *On the Coast*. London: Deutsch, 1972. Poet born Trinidad 1944, still living.

CAMPBELL, GEORGE. *First Poems*. Kingston, Jamaica: City Printery, 1945. Jamaican poet born 1918, still living.

CAREW, JAN. *Streets of Eternity*. Georgetown, Guyana: Author, 1952. Guyanese poet born 1922, still living.

CARTER, MARTIN. *The Hill of Fire Glows Red*. Miniature Poet Series. Georgetown, Guyana: Master Printery, 1951.

———. *Poems of Resistance from British Guyana*. London: Lawrence, Wishart, 1954. Guianese poet born 1927, still living.

CHAPMAN, M.J. *Barbadoes*. London: 1833. Barbados poet.

COLLYMORE, FRANK. *Collected Poems*. Bridgetown, Barbados: Advocate, 1959.

———. *Rhymed Ruminations on the Fauna of Barbados*. Bridgetown, Barbados: Advocate, 1968. Barbados poet born 1893, still living.

DALZELL, FRANK. *Moments of Leisure*. Miniature Poet Series. Georgetown, Guyana: Master Printery, 1952. Guyanese poet.

FIGUEROA, JOHN. *Blue Mountain Peak: Poetry and Prose*. Kingston, Jamaica: City Printery, 1946.

———. *Love Leaps Here*. Liverpool: Author, 1962. Jamaican poet born 1920, still living.

FORDE, A. N. *Canes by the Roadside*. Miniature Poet Series. Georgetown, Guyana: Master Printery, 1951. Guyanese poet born 1923, still living.

FRANCISCO, SLINGER "SPARROW". *Sparrow*. Radio Corporation of America. LPB - 9035.

Sparrow: Congo Man. Hilary. SP - 30006. Trinidadian calypsonian.

GRAINGER, JAMES. *Sugar Cane*. London: Whittingham 1764. Scottish poet 1723 - 1767.

HARRIS, WILSON. *Fetish*. Miniature Poet Series. Georgetown, Guyana: Master Printery, 1951.

———. *Eternity to Season*. Georgetown, Guyana: Author, 1954. Guyanese poet born 1921, still living.

HENDRIKS, A.L. *On This Mountain*. London: Deutsch, 1965.

———. *These Green Islands and Other Poems*. Kingston, Jamaica: Bolivar Press, 1971. Jamaican poet born 1922, still living.

HOLLAR, CONSTANCE. Flaming June. Kingston, Jamaica, Dawn Press, 1941. Jamaican poet. 1880 - 1945.

KEANE, ELLSWORTH MCG. *l'Oubli*. Bridgetown, Barbados: Advocate, 1950. St. Vincent poet born 1927, still living.

LAROSE, ANTHONY. *Foundations*. London: New Beacon Books, 1966. Trinidad poet born 1927, still living.

LAWRENCE, WALTER MACARTHUR. *The Poet of Guyana*. Ed. P.H. Daly. Georgetown; Guyana: Daily Chronicle, 1948. Guyanese poet. 1896 - 1942.

McAndreu, Wordsworth. *Blue Gaulding.* Miniature Poet Series. Georgetown, Guyana: Master Printery, 1958.

———. *More Poems.* Georgetown, Guyana: Author 1970. Guyanese poet born 1936, still living.

MacDermot, Thomas. *Orange Valley and Other Poems.* Kingston, Jamaica: Pioneer Press, 1951.

———. *Brown's Town and Other Poems.* Kingston, Jamaica: Jamaica Library Service, 1958. Jamaican poet. 1870 - 1933.

McFarlane, John E. Clare. *Beatrice.* Kingston, Jamaica: Jamaican Times, 1918.

———. *Poems.* Kingston, Jamaica: Gleaner, 1924.

———. *Daphne: A Tale of the Hills of St. Andrews, Jamaica.* London: Fowler Wright, 1931.

———. *Selected Shorter Poems.* Kingston, Jamaica: Jamaica Pioneer, 1954.

———. *The Magdalen: A Story of Supreme Love.* Kingston, Jamaica: Jamaica New Dawn, 1957. Jamaican poet. 1894 - 1966.

McFarlane, Roy L.C. *Hunting the Bright Stream.* Kingston, Jamaica: City Printery, 1952. Jamaican poet born 1925, still living.

McKay, Claude. *Songs of Jamaica.* Kingston, Jamaica: Gardner, 1912.

———. *Constab Ballads.* London: Watts, 1912.

———. *Spring in New Hampshire and Other Poems.* London: Grant, Richard, 1920.

———. *Harlem Shadows.* New York: Harcourt, Brace, World, 1922.

———. *Selected Poems of Claude McKay.* introd. John Dewey. New York: Bookman Associates, 1953. Jamaican poet. 1889 - 1948.

McNeill, Anthony. *Reel from "The Life Movie".* Kingston, Jamaica: Savacou, 1972. Rev. ed. 1975.

———. *Hello Ungod.* Baltimore: Peacewood Press, 1971. Jamaican poet born 1941, still living.

Marson, Una. *Tropic Reveries.* Kingston, Jamaica: Gleaner, 1930.

———. *Heights and Depths.* Kingston, Jamaica: Gleaner, 1931.

———. *The Moth and the Star.* Kingston, Jamaica: Author, 1937.

———. Towards the Stars. London: University of London, 1945. Jamaican poet. 1905 - 1965.

Martin, Egbert "Leo". *Leo's Poetical Works.* London: Collingridge, 1883.

———. *Lyrics.* Georgetown, Guyana: Baldwin, 1886. Guyanese poet. 1859 - 1887.

Morris, Mervyn. *The Pond.* London: New Beacon Books, 1973. Jamaican poet born 1937, still living.

Rattray, Carl. *Firstlings: A Collection of Poems.* Kingston, Jamaica: Author, 1950. Jamaican poet born 1929, still living.

Roberts, W. Adolphe. *Pan and Peacocks.* Boston: Four Seas, 1929. Jamaican poet 1886 - 1962.

Salkey, Andrew. *Jamaica.* London: Hutchinson, 1973. Jamaican poet born 1928, still living.

SCOTT, DENNIS. *Uncle Time*. Pittsburgh: University of Pittsburgh Press, 1973. Jamaican poet born 1939, still living.

SEYMOUR, ARTHUR J. *Verse*. Georgetown, Guyana; Author, 1937.

———. *Over Guiana Clouds*. Demerara, Guyana: Standard, 1944.

———. *The Guiana Book*. Demerara, Guyana. Argosy, 1948.

———. *Selected Poems*. Georgetown, Guyana. British Guiana Lithographic, 1965.

———. *I, Anancy*. Georgetown, Guyana; Author, 1971.

———. *Black Song*. Georgetown, Guyana: Labour Advocate, 1971.

———. *Song to Man*. Georgetown, Guyana: Labour Advocate, 1973.

———. *Italic*. Georgetown, Guyana: Labour Advocate, 1975. Guyanese poet, born 1914, still living.

SHERLOCK, PHILLIP M. *Ten Poems*. Miniature Poet Series. Georgetown: Guyana. Master Printery, 1953. Jamaican poet born 1902, still living.

TELEMAQUE, HAROLD. *Scarlet*. Miniature Poet Series. Georgetown: Guyana: Master Printery, 1953.

———. *Burnt Bush*. Port-of-Spain: Author, 1947. Trinidad poet born 1910, still living.

VIRTUE, VIVIAN. *Wings of the Morning: Poems*. Kingston, Jamaica: New Dawn, 1938. Jamaican poet born 1911, still living.

WALCOTT, DEREK. *25 Poems*. Port-of-Spain: Guardian, 1948.

———. *Epitaph for the Young*. Bridgetown, Barbados: Advocate, 1949.

———. *Poems*. Kingston, Jamaica: City Printery, 1953.

———. *In a Green Night*. London: Jonathan Cape, 1962. Cape Poetry Paperback ed. 1969.

———. *The Castaway*. London: Jonathan Cape, 1965. Cape Poetry Paperback ed. 1969.

———. *The Gulf*. London: Jonathan Cape, 1969.

———. *Selected Poems*. New York: Farrar, Straus and Giroux, 1964.

———. *Another Life*. London: Jonathan Cape, 1973. St. Lucia poet born 1930, still living.

WILLIAMS, FRANCIS. "Ode to George Haldane." In Edward Long, *History of Jamaica*. London Lowndes 1774, II, 478 - 81. Jamaican poet 1700 - 1770.

WILLIAMS, MILTON. *Pray for Rain*. Miniature Poet Series. Georgetown, Guyana: Master Printery, 1958. Guyanese poet born 1936, still living.

SECONDARY SOURCES

AIDOO, AMA ATA. "Akan and English." *West Africa* (September 21, 1968), 1099. Includes remarks on Edward Brathwaite's handling of Akan culture and language in *Masks*.

"M.J. Chapman. *Barbadoes and other Poems*." *Blackwoods Edingburgh Magazine*, 34 (October, 1833), 503 - 28. Unsigned review article: includes references to James Grainger's *Sugar Cane*.

BRATHWAITE, EDWARD. "Caribbean Critics." *New World Quarterly*, 5, 1 - 2 (1969), 5 - 12. The relationship between West Indian cultural history and effective approaches to the literature.

_____. *Folk Culture of the Slaves in Jamaica*. London: New Beacon Books, 1970. Discusses the significance of language in the cultural experience of African slaves in the New World.

_____. "Gordon Rohlehr's 'Sparrow and the Language of the Calypso'." *Caribbean Quarterly*, 14, 1 - 2 (March - June, 1968), 91 - 96. An overview of Sparrow's art as calypsonian.

BRONZ, STEPHEN H. *Roots of Negro Racial Consciousness: The 1920's: Three Harlem Renaissance Authors*. New York: Libra Books, 1964. Looks, superficially, at McKay.

BROWN, LLOYD W. "The Calypso Tradition in West Indian Literature." *Black Academy Review*, 2, 1 - 2 (Spring-Summer, 1971), 127 - 43. Examines some parallels between calypso techniques and ironic forms in the literature.

COULTHARD, GABRIEL. *Race and Colour in Caribbean Literature*. London: Oxford University Press, 1962. Useful background introduction to literature from the major language areas of the Caribbean.

DRAYTON, ARTHUR D. "West Indian Consciousness in West Indian Verse: A Historical Perspective." *Journal of Commonwealth Literature*, No. 9 (July , 1970), 66 - 88.

EMANUEL, JAMES. "The Future of Negro Poetry: A Challenge for Critics." In *Black Expression: Essays by and about Black Americans*. Ed. Addison Gayle, Jr. (New York: Weybright and Talley, 1969), pp. 100 - 09. Includes some perceptive readings of McKay's mature poetry.

FANON, FRANTZ. *Black Skin White Masks*. Trans. Charles Lam Markmann. New York: Grove, 1967. Originally published as *Peau Noire Masques Blancs*. (Paris: Editions de Seuil, 1952). Includes useful discussion of language and culture in the Caribbean (Antillean) experience.

HAMNER, ROBERT D. *V. S. Naipaul*. New York: Twayne, 1973. Preface includes discussion of the nature of West Indian literature.

HARRIS, WILSON. "Art and Criticism." *Kyk-over-al*, 3, No. 13 (December, 1951), 202 - 05.

ISMOND, PATRICIA. "Walcott versus Brathwaite." *Caribbean Quarterly*, 17, Nos. 3 - 4 (September-December, 1971), 54 - 71.

JAHN, JANHEINZ. "Poetry in Rumba." In *Introduction to African Literature*. Ed. Ulli Beier (pp. 139 - 50). Literary analysis of Caribbean folk music.

_____. *A History of Neo-African Literature: Writing in Two Continents*. Trans. Oliver Coburn and Ursula Lehrburger. London: Faber and Faber, 1966. Includes section on the calypso in the West Indies.

The Islands in Between: Essays in West Indian Literature. Louis James Ed. London: Oxford University Press, 1968. Includes discussion of the poets.

KEANE, E. McG. "Some Religious Attitudes in West Indian Poetry." *Bim*, 4, No. 15 (n. d.), 169 - 74. Deals with the earlier, post-war writers.

LAMMING, GEORGE. *The Pleasures of Exile*. London: Michael Joseph, 1960. One of the more perceptive studies of the relationship between cultural consciousness and West Indian literature.

LEWIN, OLIVE. "Jamaican Folk Music." *Caribbean Quarterly*, 14, 1 - 2 (March-June, 1968), 49 - 56.

―――. "Folk Music Research in Jamaica." In *Black Communication: Dimensions of Research and Instruction*. Ed. Jack L. Daniel (New York: Speech Communication Association, 1973) pp. 121 - 35. Looks at problems of collecting and analyzing the folk music of Jamaica.

McFARLANE, BASIL. "On Jamaican Poetry." *Kyk-over-al*, 3, No. 13 (December, 1951), 207 - 09.

McFARLANE, JOHN E. C. *A Literature in the Making*. Kingston, Jamaica: Pioneer Press, 1956. A pedestrian survey of Jamaican literature. Includes chapters on McKay, MacDermot, and Marson.

MOORE, GERALD. *The Chosen Tongue: English Writing in the Tropical World*. New York: Harper, 1970. Some useful remarks on Walcott's poetry.

OWENS, R. J. "West Indian Poetry." *Caribbean Quarterly*, 7, No. 3 (December, 1961), 120 - 27. A somewhat limited overview of the poetry.

ROHLEHR, GORDON. "Some Problems of Assessment: A Look at New Expressions in the Arts of the Contemporary Caribbean." *Caribbean Quarterly*, 17, 3 - 4 (September-December, 1971), 92 - 113. A useful background study.

VAN SERTIMA, IVAN. *Caribbean Writers: Critical Essays*. London: New Beacon Books, 1968. Includes some sketchy remarks on the major poets.

WICKHAM, JOHN. "West Indian Writing." *Bim*, 13, No. 50 (January, 1970), 68 - 80.

WYNTER, SYLVIA. "Reflections on West Indian Writing and Criticism." *Jamaica Journal*, 2, No. 4 (December, 1968), 23 - 32. An imaginatively conceived, forcefully stated essay on the need to develop insightful approaches to West Indian literature.

REFERENCES GUIDES

Barbadiana: A List of Works Pertaining to the History of the Island of Barbados. Bridgetown, Barbados: Public Library, 1966. No literary references, but the historical data include useful background readings.

Current Caribbean Bibliography. 11 vols. Port-of-Spain, Trinidad and Tobago: Caribbean Commission, 1950 - 1961. Volume seven (Ed. Berthe Canton) is a special issue, "A Bibliography of West Indian Literature: 1900 - 1957."

DELATTRE, RAE. *A Guide to Jamaican Reference Materials in the West India Reference Library.* Kingston, Jamaica: Institute of Jamaica, 1965.

ENGBER, MARJORIE. *Caribbean Fiction and Poetry.* New York: Center for Inter-American Relations, 1970.

JAHN, JANHEINZ. *A Bibliography of Neo-African Literature from Africa, America and the Caribbean.* London: Deutsch, 1965. Includes a selection of West Indian poets.

Jamaica: A Select Bibliography: 1900 - 1963. Kingston, Jamaica: Jamaica Public Library Service, 1963. Includes listing of Jamaican poets.

SANDER, REINHARD. *An Index to "Bim": 1942 - 1972.* Port-of-Spain, Trinidad and Tobago: University of the West Indies, 1973. An index of articles, poetry and other works to appear in the important West Indian literary journal.

Caribbean Acquisitions: Materials Acquired by the University of Florida. Gainesville: University of Florida, 1959 -. (Continuing publication). Lists a number of West Indian poets.

PERIODICALS

Beacon, The. Port-of-Spain, Trinidad and Tobago, 1931 - 1933. Discontinued; published some poetry.

Bim. St. Michael, Barbados, 1944 -. Current. Special issues on poetry have appeared in several years. See Reinhard Sander, *An Index to "Bim": 1942 - 1972* (1973).

Caribbean Quarterly. Department of Extra-Mural Studies, University of the West Indies, 1949 -. Current. Poetry and criticism.

Caribbean Studies. Institute of Caribbean Studies, University of Puerto Rico, 1961 -. Current. Occasional criticism.

Focus. Kingston, Jamaica. Edna Manley. Occasional publication: 1943, 1948, 1956, 1960. Discontinued. Featured poetry, criticism, and short fiction.

Jamaica Journal. Institute of Jamaica, Kingston, Jamaica, 1967 -. Current. Includes poetry and criticism from other territories as well as Jamaica.

Journal of Commonwealth Literature. University of Leeds, Leeds, England, 1965 -. Current. Criticism; annual bibliography includes West Indian poetry section.

Kaie. National History and Arts Council of Guyana, Georgetown, Guyana, 1965 - 1973. Discontinued. Included poetry.

Kyk-over-al. Georgetown, Guyana, 1945 - 1961. Discontinued. Incuded poetry and criticism.

New World Quarterly. New World Group, Kingston, Jamaica, 1964 - Current. Criticism.

Pepperpot. Kingston, Jamaica, 1951 - 1969. Discontinued. Irregular publication, featuring creative writers (including poets) from all language areas of the Caribbean.

Savacou. Savacou Publications, Kingston, Jamaica, 1970 -. Current. Criticism.

Voices. Port-of-Spain, Trinidad and Tobago, 1964 - 1966. Discontinued; featured local poets.

Index

191